Managing People

Third edition

Rosemary Thomson

Third edition revisions: Andrew Thomson

ELSEVIER
BUTTERWORTH
HEINEMANN

AMSTERDAM BOSTON HEIDELBERG LONDON NEW YORK OXFORD
PARIS SAN DIEGO SAN FRANCISCO SINGAPORE SYDNEY TOKYO

Elsevier Butterworth-Heinemann
Linacre House, Jordan Hill, Oxford OX2 8DP
30 Corporate Drive, Burlington, MA 01803

First published 1993
Second edition 1997
Third edition 2002
Reprinted 2003, 2004, 2006

British Library Cataloguing in Publication Data
A catalogue record for this book is available from the British Library

ISBN 0 7506 5618 2

For information on all Elsevier Butterworth-Heinemann
publications visit our website at www.bh.com

Working together to grow
libraries in developing countries

www.elsevier.com | www.bookaid.org | www.sabre.org

ELSEVIER   BOOK AID International   Sabre Foundation

Composition by Genesis Typesetting, Laser Quay, Rochester, Kent
Printed and bound in Great Britain by MPG Books Ltd, Bodmin, Cornwall

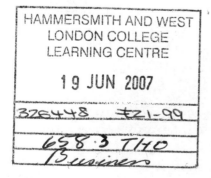

Contents

CONTENTS

Series preface from the second edition

This book is one of a series designed for people wanting to develop their capabilities as managers. You might think that there isn't anything very new in that. In one way you would be right. The fact that very many people want to learn to become better managers is not new, and for many years a wide range of approaches to such learning and development has been available. These have included courses leading to formal qualifications, organizationally-based management development programmes and a whole variety of self-study materials. A copious literature, extending from academic textbooks to sometimes idiosyncratic prescriptions from successful managers and consultants, has existed to aid – or perhaps confuse the potential seeker after managerial truth and enlightenment.

So what is new about this series? In fact, a great deal – marking in some ways a revolution in our thinking both about the art of managing and also the process of developing managers.

Where did it all begin? Like most revolutions, although there may be a single, identifiable act that precipitated the uprising, the roots of discontent are many and long-established. The debate about the performance of British managers, the way managers are educated and trained, and the extent to which shortcomings in both these areas have contributed to our economic decline, has been running for several decades.

Until recently, this debate had been marked by periods of frenetic activity – stimulated by some report or inquiry and perhaps ending in some new initiatives or policy changes – followed by relatively long periods of comparative calm. But the underlying causes for concern persisted. Basically, the majority of managers in the UK appeared to have little or no training for their role, certainly far less than their counterparts in our major competitor nations. And there was concern about the nature, style and appropriateness of the management education and training that was available.

The catalyst for this latest revolution came in late 1986 and early 1987, when three major reports reponed the whole issue. The 1987 reports were *The Making of British Managers* by John Constable and Roger McCormick, carried out for the British Institute of Management and the CBI, and *The Making of Managers* by Charles Handy, carried out for the (then) Manpower Services Commission, National

Economic Development Office and British Institute of Management. The 1986 report, which often receives less recognition than it deserves as a key contribution to the recent changes, was *Management Training: context and process* by Iain Mangham and Mick Silver, carried out for the Economic and Social Research Council and the Department of Trade and Industry. It is not the place to review in detail what the reports said. Indeed, they and their consequences are discussed in several places in this series of books. But essentially they confirmed that:

- British managers were undertrained by comparison with their counterparts internationally.
- The majority of employers invested far too little in training and developing their managers.
- Many employers found it difficult to specify with any degree of detail just what it was was they required successful managers to be able to do.

The Constable/McCormick and Handy reports advanced various recommendations for addressing these problems, involving an expansion of management education and development, a reformed structure of qualifications and a commitment from employers to a code of practice for management development. While this analysis was not new, and had echoes of much that had been said in earlier debates, this time a few leading individuals determined that the response should be both radical and permanent. The response was coordinated by the newly-established Council for Management Education and Development (now the National Forum for Management Education and Development (NFMED)) under the energetic and visionary leadership of Bob (now Sir Bob) Reid formerly of Shell UK and the British Railways Board.

Under the umbrella of NFMED a series of employer-led working parties tackled the problem of defining what it was that managers should be able to do, and how this differed for people at different levels in their organizations; how this satisfactory ability to perform might be verified; and how an appropriate structure of management qualifications could be put in place. This work drew upon the methods used to specify vocational standards in industry and commerce, and led to the development and introduction of competence-based management standards and qualifications. In this context, competence is defined as the ability to perform the activities within an occupation or function to the standards expected in employment.

It is this competence-based approach that is new in our thinking about the manager's capabilities. It is also what is new about this series of books, in that they are designed to support both this new structure of management standards, and of development activities based on it. The series was originally commissioned to support the Institute of Management's Certificate and Diploma qualifications, which were one of the first to be based on the new standards. However, these books are equally appropriate to any university, college or indeed company course leading to a certificate in management or diploma in management studies.

The standards were specified through an extensive process of consultation with a large number of managers in organizations of many different types and sizes. They are therefore employment-based and employer-supported. And they fill the gap that Mangham and Silver identified – now we do have a language to described what it is employers want their managers to be able to do – at least in part.

If you are engaged in any form of management development leading to a certificate or diploma qualification conforming to the national management standards, then you are probably already familiar with most of the key ideas on which the standards are based. To achieve their key purpose, which is defined as achieving the organization's objectives and continuously improving its performance, managers need to perform four key roles: managing operations, managing finance, managing people and managing information. Each of these key roles has a substructure of units and elements, each with associated performance and assessment criteria.

The reason for the qualification 'in part' is that organizations are different, and jobs within them are different. Thus the generic management standards probably do not cover all the management competencies that you may need to possess in your job. There are almost certainly additional things, specific to your own situation in your own organization, that you need to be able to do. The standards are necessary, but almost certainly not sufficient. Only you, in discussion with your boss, will be able to decide what other capabilities you need to possess. But the standards are a place to start, a basis on which to build. Once you have demonstrated your proficiency against the standards, it will stand you in good stead as you progress through your organization, or change jobs.

So how do the new standards change the process by which you develop yourself as a manager? They change the process of development, or of gaining a management qualification, quite a lot. It is no longer a question of acquiring information and facts, perhaps by being 'taught' in some classroom environment, and then being tested to see what you can recall. It involves demonstrating, in a quite specific way, that you can do certain things to a particular standard of performance. And because of this, it puts a much greater onus on you to manage your own development, to decide how you can demonstrate any particular competence, what evidence you need to present, and how you can collect it. Of course, there will always be people to advise and guide you in this, if you need help.

But there is another dimension, and it is to this that this series of books is addressed. While the standards stress ability to perform, they do not ignore the traditional knowledge base that has been associated with management studies. Rather, they set this in a different context. The standards are supported by 'underpinning knowledge and understanding' which has three components:

- Purpose and context, which is knowledge and understanding of the manager's objectives, and of the relevant organizational and environmental influences, opportunities and values.
- Principles and methods which is knowledge and understanding of the theories, models, principles, methods and techniques that provide the basis of competent managerial performance.
- Data, which is knowledge and understanding of specific facts likely to be of importance to meeting the standards.

Possession of the relevant knowledge and understanding underpinning the standards is needed to support competent managerial performance as specified in the standards. It also has an important role in supporting the transferability of management capabilities. It helps to ensure that you have done more than learned 'the way we do things around here' in your own organization. It indicates a recognition of the wider things which underpin competence, and that you will be able to change jobs or organizations and still be able to perform effectively.

These books cover the knowledge and understanding underpinning the management standards, most specifically in the category of principles and methods. But their coverage is not limited to the minimum required by the standards, and extends in both depth and breadth in many areas. The authors have tried to approach these underlying principles and methods in a practical way. They use many short cases and examples which we hope will demonstrate how, in practice, the principles and methods, and knowledge of purpose and context plus data, support the ability to perform as required by the management standards. In particular we hope that this type of presentation will enable you to identify and learn from similar examples in your own managerial work.

You will already have noticed that one consequence of this new focus on the standards is that the traditional 'functional' packages of knowledge and theory do not appear. The standard textbook titles such as 'quantitative methods', 'production management', 'organization behaviour', etc. disappear. Instead, principles and methods have been collected together in clusters that more closely match the key roles within the standards. You will also find a small degree of overlap in some of the volumes, because some principles and methods support several of the individual units within the standards. We hope you will find this a useful reinforcement.

Having described the positive aspects of standards-based management development, it would be wrong to finish without a few cautionary remarks. The developments described above may seem simple, logical and uncontroversial. It did not always seem that way in the years of work which led up to the introduction of the standards. To revert to the revolution analogy, the process has been marked by ideological conflict and battles of sovereignty and territory. It has sometimes been unclear which side various parties are on – and indeed how many sides there are! The revolution, if well advanced, is not at an end. Guerrilla warfare continues in parts of the territory.

Perhaps the best way of describing this is to say that, which competence-based standards are widely recognized as at least a major part of the answer to improving managerial performance, they are not the whole answer. There is still some debate about the way competencies are defined, and whether those in the standards are most appropriate on which to base assessment of managerial performance. There are other models of management competencies than those in the standards.

There is also a danger in separating management performance into a set of discrete components. The whole is, and needs to be, more than the sum of the parts. Just like bowling an off-break in cricket, practising a golf swing or forehand drive in tennis, you have to combine all the separate movements into a smooth, flowing action. How you combine the competencies, and build on them, will mark your own individual style as a manager.

We should also be careful not to see the standards as set in stone. They determine what today's managers need to be able to do. As the arena in which managers operate changes, then so will the standards. The lesson for all of us as managers is that we need to go on learning and developing, acquiring new skills or refining existing ones. Obtaining your certificate or diploma is like passing a milepost, not crossing the finishing line.

All the changes and developments of recent years have brought management qualifications, and the processes by which they are gained, much closer to your job as a manager. We hope these books support this process by providing bridges between your own experience and the underlying principles and methods which will help you to demonstrate your competence. Already, there is a lot of evidence that managers enjoy the challenge of demonstrating competence, and find immediate benefits in their jobs from the programmes based on these new-style qualifications. We hope you do too. Good luck in your career development.

Paul Jervis

Acknowledgements

This third edition has been prepared by Andrew Thomson, husband of Rosemary, who very sadly died in 1998. But the concept, the structure, the style and the spirit of the book are still hers, and it is therefore still very much her book.

The author acknowledges ideas and concepts contained in Open University Business School courses, in particular 'The Effective Manager'. Several of the examples of both good and bad practice in this book have been reported in *People Management*, the journal of the Chartered Institute of Personnel and Development and published in Personnel Publications Ltd.

CHAPTER 1

Managing people in the twenty-first century

INTRODUCTION

Managing people is the most complex dimension of management, and arguably one which is most difficult to learn, especially for line managers who also have other responsibilities. In this chapter, we are going to take an overview of what a manager needs to understand in relation to managing people in a changing environment, as well as looking at the predominant models of managing people. The theme of the chapter is change, but we will also comment on the importance of continuity and context. We will be looking at the following issues:

- What does a manager do?
- Trends in environmental change
- Trends in organizational change
- Trends in managerial skills
- Continuity
- Approaches to managing people

    The objectives of the organization
    Ethical considerations for managers
    Historical phases of people management
    Human Resource Management

- The importance of context
- The impact of people management practices

- What is 'good' human relations?
- How to use this book.

WHAT DOES A MANAGER DO?

At the end of this chapter, you will be asked to undertake a diary exercise to try to define what you do in your job as a manager. Listing your key responsibilities as they may be defined in your job description is one way – but how do you classify what you do on a day-to-day basis? What was the first managerial task you undertook this morning? Could you relate it clearly to one of your key responsibilities?

Catherine works as a junior manager in the Banking Section of the Cashier's Department in a Regional Authority. She lists as her key responsibility the banking of all monies received in the Region. This involves supervising clerks who sort out cash, cheques and Giro pay-in slips by location and check these against control sheets. She is responsible for checking any discrepancies in the daily total and informing other departments responsible for errors. However, the first thing she did one morning was to confirm the holiday rota with her staff; on another morning, she had to spend some time training a new recruit to the Section and then attend a monthly meeting on staff appraisal in the Authority; on yet another morning, she had to talk to one of the clerks about persistent lateness . . . and so on. None of these tasks closely related to her key responsibility, yet they were all part of her job.

Surprising though it may seem, what managers do is a matter of considerable uncertainty, in spite of great deal of research. Mintzberg showed from activity studies that a manager's job is characterized by a considerable fragmentation of varied and brief activities, with frequent interruptions. Managers prefer verbal contacts, although also having to deal with substantial amounts of papers, and a lot of their time is spent in meetings, some unscheduled. Pressure is created by the pace at which these activities are conducted. There is little time for reflection, and managers tend to operate to short-term rather than long-term objectives.

One way of looking at your role as a manager is to classify what you do into the elements of the job. Henri Fayol, a mining engineer by training, spent his working life in a French mining and metallurgical combine, first as an engineer and then moving into general manage-

ment, finally becoming managing director. From his prolonged observation of managers, he concluded that every managerial job contained the same five elements, although individual managers in
different industries might lay more stress on some elements than
on others. Fayol's five elements of management were:

- *Forecasting and planning* – looking to the future; ensuring the
  objectives of the organization are being met; short- and long-
  term forecasting; being able to adapt plans as circumstances
  change; attempting to predict what is going to happen.
- *Organizing* – ensuring that the structure of the organization
  allows its basic activities to be carried out; giving direction;
  defining responsibilities; making decisions and backing these
  up by an efficient system for selecting and training staff.
- *Commanding* – we might prefer to use the word 'leading' here
  since this refers to the relationship between a manager and
  his or her staff in relation to the task being performed including counselling, appraisal, giving feedback, allocating work
  and so on.
- *Coordinating* – ensuring that individuals, teams and departments work in harmony towards common organizational
  goals; keeping all activities in perspective with regard to
  the overall aims of the organization.
- *Controlling* – ensuring that the other four elements are being
  carried out; operating sanctions if necessary (Pugh and
  Hickson, 1996).

Catherine's early morning activities could readily have been classified
into these elements. The holiday rota involved forecasting and planning as well as coordination; the training session required organizing
as did the staff appraisal system; commanding and controlling were
involved in her talk with the person who was not performing adequately.

Although Fayol undertook his research earlier this century and his
book *Administration Industrielle et Generale* was first published in 1916,
his framework for looking at what a manager does is still valid today.

More recent approaches to what managers do have been through
competences, whether functional or behavioural. Britain now has a
system of occupational standards at five different levels subdivided
into key roles, units, and elements of tasks derived from functional
analysis, and competence involves not only vocational skills, but the
knowledge and understanding which underpins them. This book is

designed to be compatible with a Level 4 National Vocational Qualification in Management, and especially several of the units in the Managing People key role:

C5   Develop productive working relationships
C8   Select personnel for activities
C10 Develop teams and individuals to enhance performance
C15 Respond to poor performance in the team

The occupational competences are focused on the job being carried out, while behavioural competences are related to the behaviours of the manager. Richard Boyatzis (1982), in his book *The Competent Manager*, analysed these behaviours within five main clusters: goal and action management; leadership; human resource management; directing subordinates; and focus on others. The human resource management cluster, the most relevant for this book, consists of four competences: use of socialized power; positive regard; managing group process; and accurate self-assessment.

Since this seminal work, many organizations have defined their own desired behaviours, using a similar profiling approach (and often more easily understandable terms).

The majority of large organizations and many medium and smaller ones have adopted one of these competence-based approaches to management job definition and from that linked it to training and, indeed, in many organizations, to a range of other aspects of managing people such as recruitment, induction, staff appraisal and promotion.

Investigate   Does your organization have a formal policy on management training and development?
    Does your organization adopt a competence-based approach to training?

TRENDS IN ENVIRONMENTAL CHANGE

The research by Fayol and the more recent work on competences is based on observation of what managers actually do. While this is perfectly valid and gives us an indication of the skills needed to perform a managerial job, it does not tell us about the skills needed for the future. The reason that skills will need to change is that the environment itself is changing and will continue to do so, arguably at a faster rate than ever before in human history, to which organizations, managers and workforces will need to respond. Some of the key changes are:

- Globalization is increasing competitive pressures such that competition is no longer internal to a country but with organizations far across the world.
- The growing importance, especially in the economic and regulatory areas, of Britain being a member of the European Union. If Britain joins the Euro, this trend will be further enhanced.
- New technologies, especially those in the area of IT, are changing the nature of work itself.
- New working practices and policies are derived from abroad. Of particular relevance to this book, many aspects of Human Resource Management (HRM) have been borrowed from the United States.
- The pressures of financial markets has meant that organizations have to give primary attention to shareholder value, arguably to the detriment of stakeholder values.
- Performance management will increasingly seek to integrate the various aspects of HRM with the goals of the organization.
- Demographic trends mean more women, an older average age, and greater cultural diversity in the labour force.
- There will also be more atypical workers with increasing flexibility in hours and through teleworking.
- Careers in the sense of spending most of one's working life at a single job for the same employer are being replaced by working for a number of employers and for many, at a number of different jobs.
- Developing different skills requires lifelong learning, and a degree of initiative about personal development.
- Skills and training are increasingly defined through competences, whether through occupational standards defined by functional analysis or behavioural competences.
- Within managerial roles, there is an increasing emphasis on leadership and the ability to bring about change rather than management in the sense of organizing a stable if complex situation.
- There is a move away from collective relations between employers and their workforce to legal rights for individuals.

TRENDS IN ORGANIZATIONAL CHANGE

The number of management layers has been decreasing.

- There has been an increased delegation of responsibility throughout the workforce, with more workers carrying out at least some managerial roles.
- Pay is being linked more directly to performance and/or results.
- More work is being undertaken in multidisciplinary teams.
- Managers are undertaking continuous learning rather than periodic training, and more development overall.
- Managers have a wider span of control, including responsibility for people who are widely dispersed, supported by the use of IT.
- There is an increasing responsibility for line managers in the management of people, with HR staff being reduced to a support role.
- There is a move to generalist rather than specialist managers.
- There is extensive contracting out with organizations retaining a smaller core of permanent workers.
- Organizations would become less diversified, retaining only those parts of the business which were key to adding value.

Investigate   How far are these changes true of your organization?

TRENDS IN MANAGERIAL SKILLS

Surveys on expectations for the future have identified two kinds of skills – those which were concerned with the external environment of the organization and those which were concerned with its internal operations.

Management skills which were concerned with the external environment included:

- Being change-oriented and proactive in sensing and predicting change.
- Being capable of strategic thinking – looking at the whole picture.

6

- Being capable of 'thinking on their feet' and good at making decisions quickly.
- Being aware of and taking account of the different stake-holders in the organization of the future where new and complex relationships such as partners, alliances, joint ventures and so on were likely to become more commonplace.
- Managing risk and tolerating failure.

Skills related to internal management included:

- Coping with change and flexibility; responding to and managing change.
- Demonstrating commitment to the organization and high energy levels to help them cope with increased workloads and pressures.
- Being aware of the organization as a whole, not just the bits with which the manager is concerned on a day-to-day basis.
- Building and developing teams.
- Taking responsibility for their own development and learning.
- Financial skills.
- Skills in information management and IT.

In addition to these skills related to the external and internal environments of the organization, managers would also need to have a concern for total quality management and be able to operate effectively in the international environment.

There is insufficient space in the book to give all the changes noted above the attention they deserve, but they need to be appreciated as part of the context within which management in the twenty-first century will take place. The last chapter deals explicitly with the implications of change as a process, but change is also a theme throughout the rest of the book. We will be reminding you of the need to develop yourself and your staff, to update existing skills and acquire new ones if you are to survive as a manager in the new millennium.

CONTINUITY

Having noted the prevalence of change, however, a cautionary point needs to be made. There is still a great deal of continuity; many aspects of human relations remain the same today as they have done for thousands of years since organizations became important in human evolution. What then remains the same? Essentially human behaviour, and it is an appreciation of what lies behind this which is at the heart of the successful management of people. Managing people is not just about making decisions and giving orders. To get the best out of them, managers need to understand the point of view of the people involved. Not only this, but they need to understand what lies behind this point of view. Obviously people are different, have different values and objectives and may behave differently even in the same situation. But there are also social pressures in a group which predispose people to think and behave similarly. It is this recognition of the way individuals act as individuals but also relate to groups and social pressures which managers need to understand. Organizations and their contexts may be changing but the essence of the relationships between people remains the same.

APPROACHES TO MANAGING PEOPLE

It will be helpful for you to know something about the different approaches to managing people, and indeed to be aware of the underlying assumptions in this book. It is also important for you as a manager to know what the organization's expectations of you will be in terms of managing people, even though you may not be, indeed are unlikely to be, a personnel specialist.

The objectives of organizations

One of the most difficult issues for managers is the extent to which ethical considerations play a part, both at the individual level and at the organizational one. At the organizational level there are two conflicting perspectives. One school of thought argues that the shareholders' interests as the owners of the organization are the only ones which should be taken into account. Moreover, the organization will thrive or not according to whether it can please the financial markets which essentially reflect shareholder interests. Its capacity to raise capital, to prevent itself from being taken over, and to invest in the future will be dependent on whether it makes a satisfactory level of profits which can repay the shareholders' investment. If managers do not achieve these objectives they are likely to be sacked and replaced by others who conform more to shareholders' interests. In addition, market pressures appear to push in the same direction, such that higher efficiencies and competitive advantage are focused towards the main goal of profitability. Not to do this will result in competitive decline and ultimately collapse.

The other main perspective is the stakeholder approach, which argues that a range of those affected by the operations of the organization have a legitimate interest in policies and decisions, and that account should therefore be taken of these. Those with such interests would certainly include the owners and also the employees, the customers, the suppliers, the governments under which the organization is regulated, the communities where it operates, and increasingly the wider environment. Very often stakeholders can exert pressure on an organization and become a constraint on managerial choice; social legitimacy is an important concern even for very large organizations. A few years ago, Shell was constrained by public opinion in what it could do in disposing of its oil rigs, and was effectively prevented from dumping them at sea, and there are many equivalent examples. The solution as between the interests of shareholders and different groups of stakeholders lies in the definition of priorities as between them. This is usually a pragmatic judgement, and the balance may well change over time. Financial concerns may be uppermost in organizational objectives, but they cannot be exclusive.

Investigate   Identify clashes between stakeholders in your organization.

Ethical considerations for managers

At the individual level do managers have to follow the expectations of their employer to the extent of ignoring any ethical considerations? But few organizations have absolute rules which dictate all courses of action. Most are political entities in which decisions are significantly decentralized. Moreover, it is not always clear what is the most economically or financially advantageous course of action. For that matter, managers would not be managers if they did not have some discretion in decision-making over some parts of their responsibilities; one of these parts is likely to be in the way they manage people. What are the perspectives that guide behaviour? Some are:

- Acting in accordance with explicit rules.
- Acting out of a sense of justice or equality.

- Acting in what is perceived to be the most efficient or effective way.
- Acting because of orders to follow a certain approach.
- Acting because it is what others do.
- Acting under pressure from interest groups.
- Acting in one's personal self-interest or that of another group to which one belongs.
- Acting to satisfy one's conscience.
- Acting in a way which is most beneficial for most people.

All of these might be considered legitimate rationalizations for action, but none of them are likely to satisfy everyone. Most decisions must be tradeoffs between different considerations and will tend to favour one set of interests rather than another. Ethical behaviour in this context is thus more a matter of having a consistent moral approach than it is making clear distinctions between right and wrong.

Historical phases of people management

Another approach to thinking about the management of people is by looking at the extent of change over time; historically, there have been several phases in the way in which the management of people has been structured:

The welfarist phase, in which employers saw their role as extending to caring for the moral and physical needs of their workers. This may have been said to start with Robert Owen at the onset of the Industrial Revolution, but is more commonly associated with the views of better employers, especially those of a Quaker background, in the later nineteenth and early twentieth centuries. The Institute of Welfare Workers was founded in 1913 as the first association for those involved in this functional area.

The industrial efficiency phase post World War I, comprising elements of scientific management, in which people were seen to be the key to efficiency if their work was properly structured and analyzed. The name of the Institute of Welfare workers was changed to that of the Institute of Labour Management in 1931 to reflect the changing perspective.

The personnel administration phase from the late 1930s to the late 1950s. As the role widened from the management of work to the management of people and became more bureaucratized, the administration of the function became more important. This was also a period which saw the influence of the American 'human relations' school and recognition of the contribution of the behavioural sciences, notably sociology and psychology. Again there was a change in title of the leading professional institute with the change in 1946 from Institute of Labour management to Institute of Personnel Management.

The industrial relations phase from the late 1950s into the 1970s. During this period the key issue relating to people at work was that of managing employment relations, especially through collective bargaining with unions. Issues of control over working practices, productivity, and new technology meant that management was challenged by the unions in respect of what many managers saw as management prerogatives. Increasingly the state also became involved in areas such as health and safety, sex and race discrimination, training, and employment contracts and the rights of individual workers at work.

The professionalization of personnel management began in the 1970s with the spread of new ideas and the more rapid growth of consultancy in a range of areas connected with people, especially as concern grew over absenteeism, high turnover, and the lack of motivation in the workforce. Employers sought to respond by more participative policies, including job enrichment and job enlargement and self-managed groups. There was a growth in the influence of the Institute of Personnel Management, which later merged with the Institute of Training and development to form the Institute of Personnel and Development.

Human Resource Management (HRM)

The most recent phase, from the late 1980s, has been the growth of Human Resource Management, which as with so many ideas in industry, had its origins in the United States. You will have noticed the term Human Resource Management (HRM) being used above, and you will almost certainly have heard about it in your daily work or in previous reading. It is now the predominant framework in current usage, even though by no means always implemented in the way the purists would like, so what does it mean? The following perspectives are taken from Storey (2001)

1 Beliefs and assumptions:
    ■ That it is human resources which give competitive edge.
    ■ That the aim should be not mere compliance with rules, but employee commitment.

■ That employees should be very carefully selected and developed.

2 Strategic qualities:
 ■ Because of the above factors, HR decisions are of strategic importance.
 ■ Top management involvement is necessary.
 ■ HR policies should be integrated into business strategy – stemming from it and if possible contributing to it.

3 Critical role of managers:
 ■ Because HR practice is critical to the core activities of the business, it is too important to be left to HR specialists alone.
 ■ Line managers need to be closely involved as both deliverers and drivers of the HR policies.
 ■ Much greater attention is paid to the management of managers themselves.

4 Key levers:
 ■ Managing culture is more important than managing systems and procedures.
 ■ Integrated action on selection, communication, training, rewards, and development.
 ■ Restructuring and job design to allow devolved responsibility and empowerment.

Another way of looking at HRM is to see it as a cycle of relationships, as in Figure 1.1. This is essentially a system model of human

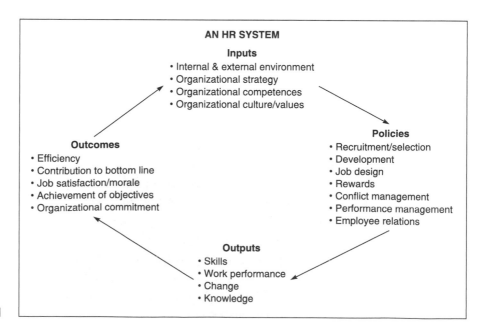

Figure 1.1

aspects of an organization. But it needs to be noted that while the arrows indicate a causal impact of each dimension upon the one succeeding it, this is only partial. Thus the inputs are the most important influence on the policies, but they are not the sole determining influence. There will be other dimensions, such as the contribution of particular individuals. This is true all the way round, and indeed in the last link in the loop, the effect of outcomes of the HR system on the inputs, can only be very limited. Nevertheless, it is important to think of people management as a system, not just a set of disparate activities.

A further consideration about HRM is the extent of its coverage. There have been several answers to this, but one which provides a broad scope is Gospel's (1992) categorization of three different sorts of relations, namely:

- Work relations, which encompasses the way in which work is organized and the deployment of workers around production systems and technologies.
- Employment relations, which deals with arrangements governing essentially individual dimension of recruitment and selection, reward systems, and job tenure and promotion.
- Industrial relations, which is concerned with representational and participation systems in an organization.

How does HRM differ from its main predecessor, personnel management? Some of the differences are implied above, namely: a more important role for personnel specialists in setting policy; a lesser role for either top management or line managers; less integration of the various personnel sub-functions such as rewards or development; and less integration with the overall business strategy. While people are important, they are not necessarily as important as with the HRM assumptions. There is also a third school of managing people, which is almost by default in that people are not given a major role in the philosophy of the business. Rather there is little training, low wages, little discretion for employees, no career patterns, and a general hire and fire approach in which people are very much secondary to short-term financial results. It is not quite clear where companies that are outsourcing some or all of their HR activities fit in this categorization, but it is a trend which has been growing and looks likely to continue to grow. At the end of 2001, two-thirds of UK organizations said in a survey they were outsourcing at least some of the HR function.

Cable and Wireless is outsourcing the bulk of its HR function in order to save an estimated £13m by 2005. This is in spite of the fact that organization to which the outsourcing is being sub-contracted, epeopleserve, is half owned by its main competitor, British Telecom.

Investigate   Which approach to managing people does your employer subscribe to?

In this book, the underlying assumptions will be that of the HRM approach, as the most up-to-date and people-focused of the three main approaches. It is also the one which emphasizes your role as a manager in the management of people. But it may well be that your own organization does not subscribe to the HRM approach, or does so to only a partial extent. Indeed it would be quite unrealistic to see the HRM approach as dominant in practice. There is a sense in which the rhetoric of HRM has outstripped the reality, and that other priorities dictated by competitive market pressures, such as restructuring, outsourcing, delayering, takeovers or mergers may take precedence over HR aspirations. Reality is a mixed model, with many organizations having elements of two or even all three of the types mentioned above, and changing practice at different times. It would also be wrong to argue that there is any one set of universal best practices. What is best for the organization may differ for a number of reasons, not least the context in which it finds itself, and we need to appreciate this dimension, as outlined below.

THE IMPORTANCE OF CONTEXT

As with the point about continuity above, we need to note the importance of context, or what is often referred to as a contingency-based approach to management. Managing people, like other aspects of management or indeed other aspects of human behaviour, is subject to debate and disagreement. Different theories have been advanced and research carried out with different implications about almost all the topics in the book. This book does not take a specific stand on these, although it does frequently quote research, but rather attempts to take a middle ground. There is one exception to this, and one which would actually be agreed by most observers. This is that almost all situations are different, whether in time, technology, markets, or structure; issues of managing people are contingent on the situation and almost always provide a range of choices rather than a single solution.

Managing people is not something for which prescriptive guidelines can be provided irrespective of the context. Product and labour markets, the prevailing technology, the structure of the organization, including its management hierarchy, all create some constraints on the HR policies. Small companies may have more intimate interpersonal relations than large companies, which may be a good or a bad thing. Companies which are driven by the needs of the production line require a different management of people from those where the skills required are creative and individualistic. Those which are in a growth phase and there is general optimism produce different interpersonal relations to those where there is decline, and survival and job insecurity are the order of the day. Culture matters too. We shall look later at different cultures between countries, but cultures can vary considerably between organizations even in similar industries, according to leadership, traditions and the underlying value system. Managing people must take account of these dimensions, as well as the individuals and groups that make up most of the content of this book. What we would like to argue, however, is that while context may be important, it is not a completely over-riding constraint; there is always an element of choice for organizations in what they do.

THE IMPACT OF PEOPLE MANAGEMENT PRACTICES

One question which you may have been asking yourself is how does managing people contribute to the success of the organization, and especially the bottom line? This is currently one of the key areas of research in the human resources field, and while there are no absolutely definitive results, there are increasing indications that there is a positive relationship between 'good' HR practices and organizational results. The largest survey has been by Huselid (1995) in the United States, who analyzed the impact of 13 'high-performance work practices' and found that firms utilizing these had significantly lower turnover, higher staff productivity, and better financial performance in both the short and long run than firms that did not utilize them. In Britain, Fox and McLeay (1991) found that the return on capital of a firm with a higher degree of integration between the HR function and corporate strategy could be expected to be substantially above the average for its sector. Patterson et al. (1997) in research at the

Institute of Work Psychology concluded that employee commitment and a positive psychological contract are fundamental to improving performance, with job design and the acquisition of skills, including selection, induction, and the use of appraisals, being particularly important. Guest et al. (2000) echoed these findings about a positive psychological contract and also found that an informal climate of employee involvement and consultation appears to have an important influence on performance. These findings are now becoming cumulatively convincing, but the doubters would probably still like a definitive survey which brings all the various components together.

WHAT IS 'GOOD' PEOPLE MANAGEMENT?

There can be no complete answer to this question. There are ethical, political, and operational dimensions. But in recent years a good deal of attention has been given to trying to identify 'high performance work systems', which get the best out of people working at the organization. Again, what precisely should constitute such systems is itself a matter of some controversy, but the US Department of Labor has suggested the following:

- Careful and extensive systems for recruitment, selection and training.
- Formal systems for sharing information with those who work in the organization.
- Clear job design.
- Local level participation procedures.
- Monitoring of attitudes.
- Performance appraisals.
- Properly functioning grievance procedures.
- Promotion and compenzation procedures that provide for the recognition and financial rewarding of high performing members of the workforce.

HOW TO USE THIS BOOK

This book has been written to give managers the essential knowledge and understanding which will underpin their competence in managing people in practice. This involves knowledge of some of the more important research in the area and of recent developments, but it also involves recognition of what is 'good practice' in the management of people. Examples of practice, good and bad, are given throughout in the ruled sections within each chapter; most of this information is in the public domain and can be found in any newspaper or professional journal.

The contents list and the index will give you an idea of the coverage of the subject area, so you can use the book as a reference when you want to find out more about a particular idea or set of skills. Or you can read it through from beginning to end since it is not designed to be an 'academic' text.

Each chapter consists of an introduction, setting the scene for what is to come. The main section covers research, ideas and practical examples of various topics within the subject area. It also contains a number of points where you are asked to stop reading and think about how the ideas relate to practice in your own organization. These points are indicated by the word 'INVESTIGATE', since they are designed to involve you in finding out about how or why things happen in your workplace. Where appropriate, some guidelines about relevant legal and regulatory frameworks are included.

At the end of each chapter there is a summary of the main content and some activities which you might like to try out to check your understanding of what you have read or how you might apply some of the ideas in your own job. Finally, you can find a list of books on the subject which you might like to read if you want to find out more about a particular aspect of managing people in the section on further reading after the bibliography at the end of the book.

Summary

This chapter has introduced you to what managers do in their everyday jobs and the skills they will need to meet the challenges and opportunities of managing in the twenty-first century if their organizations are to succeed. It has also introduced a framework of approaches to managing people, with particular attention to Human Resource Management (HRM), the predominant approach in the current literature, and has noted both the research on the impact of human relations on organizational performance and provided a list of what might be considered good human relations practices.

Activities

1   *Your role as a manager* Over the next few days, try to keep a 'diary' of what you actually do in your job. You might find it useful to use the headings devised by Fayol for classifying the elements of management. You might need to keep a 'miscellaneous' heading for those tasks which do not immediately fall into Fayol's classification.

2   Go through the list of skills which have been identified as necessary for the managers of the future. Identify those which you need to update and those which you need to acquire. Against each of these, note down some suggestions for how you can update or learn new skills.

CHAPTER 2

Managing yourself

INTRODUCTION

The purpose of this book is about the management of people and, indeed, the American theorist, Harold Koontz stated that 'Managing is the art of getting things done through and with people in formally organized groups.' However, an anonymous writer has been attributed with the statement that 'Management is the art of getting other people to do all the work.' Whichever of these statements appeals to you, the fact is that, as a manager, you cannot do everything yourself. And, unless you can manage yourself – your time, your workload and so on – you are unlikely to be an effective manager of others.

In this chapter we will be looking at various aspects of managing yourself, including:

- Managing your time.
- Delegating.
- Planning your workload.
- Making decisions.
- Active listening.
- Communicating.
- Counselling.
- Developing yourself.
- Managing your manager.

MANAGING YOUR TIME

Do you know just how much your time is worth? Try the following exercise and you may surprise yourself.

Investigate

- ■ Annual salary   . . . .
- ■ Add 25% (Health, Pension Fund,
  National Insurance etc.)   . . . .
- ■ Add 100% for overheads (office, light,
  heat, computer services, administration,
  secretarial services, travel etc.)   . . . .
- ■ Add any commissions and/or
  allowances, value of company car,
  healthcare plan etc.   . . . .

TOTAL   . . . .
- ■ Divide total by the number of
  working days per year (less holiday
  and weekends)   . . . .
- ■ Divide result by eight (hours per day)   . . . .
- ■ Divide result by 60 (minutes per hour)   . . . .

(*From The Effective Manager, Open University Business School*)

If you carried out the exercise, never mind how roughly, you should have a monetary figure for how much you are worth to your organization per minute. Although this may seem a rather commercial way to view yourself, it should make you realize just what wasted time can cost you and your company.

John Adair (1987) suggests there are five main ways in which managers waste time. These are:

- ■ Procrastinating.
- ■ Mismanaging paperwork.
- ■ Holding unnecessary meetings.
- ■ Failing to set priorities.
- ■ Delegating ineffectively.

People often procrastinate because a particular piece of work is boring or unpleasant. One solution to this is to set aside one hour a day – often the first hour at work – to deal with all the jobs you would like to put off. Not only does this ensure the jobs are done but it can result in feelings of satisfaction and achievement at having completed them.

Even in this age of computers, there still seems to be an inordinate amount of paperwork which comes across a manager's desk; and, in some cases, it stays there or is simply moved to another pile. One suggestion which can help managers who find themselves pushing paper around is to resolve never to pick up a piece of paper and put it down without doing something with it. And to set aside some time each day to file papers, even if they are 'filed' in the waste bin.

> A senior engineer in a construction company found his workplace became very untidy very quickly because there were always a large number of projects being undertaken at any one time. He was fairly efficient at dealing with the paperwork as it came in, but usually failed to get around to filing the project folders after use. As a result, they piled up on his desk and he would waste time looking for the right one when he needed it. He realized this was an inefficient use of his time and gave some thought to the problem. He realized that the reason he didn't get around to filing the project folders was because the filing cabinet was across the room and it was easier to let them pile up than to walk a few yards to file them. By moving the filing cabinet next to his desk, the problem was solved; the folders were automatically filed as he finished with them and he could always find them quickly when he needed them.

Managers can spend a lot of time in meetings, and these meetings are not always productive. Think back to the exercise you carried out to assess how much your time is worth per minute – and how many minutes in a working week you spend in meetings, both formal and informal. There is often a strong argument for evaluating and re-evaluating the reasons for holding meetings and asking questions such as, 'Why are we holding this meeting and what would happen if we didn't hold it?' as well as thinking about less time-consuming ways of communicating with others such as through electronic mail.

Setting priorities is an integral part of planning your workload. Like many managers, you may have several projects to look after at a time; some are likely to be more or less urgent than others. Spending time on a daily or weekly basis prioritizing jobs for yourself and your team should help you to ensure that the more urgent jobs are carried out first and that valuable time is not wasted on less urgent work which could be delegated or routinized.

Other time-wasting occurrences include:

- Dealing with unwanted visitors.
- Telephone interruptions.
- Social chit-chat.
- Travelling.
- Dealing with other people's problems.

Spending a little time thinking about each of these and how such wasted time can be prevented is a worthwhile use of your time. For example, if you have a secretary, maybe he or she could deal with visitors and filter your telephone calls. Make specific times when you cannot be disturbed by 'phone or callers. Use travelling time to and from work productively; in other cases, write or telephone instead of calling in person or see if someone else can go. Encourage people to think about solutions to their problems before coming to you for help in deciding what they should do.

Investigate   Be honest with yourself – do you waste time in any of the ways suggested by Adair? If so, take some time to consider how you could save time and waste less of it.

DELEGATION

'Effective delegation is an essential part of a manager's job. Delegating is easy; it is the "effective" part which is the tricky bit!' (Manager on a training course)

Delegation does not, and should not, be used as an excuse to pass on the more boring work to your staff. This will not motivate them, nor play a part in their development. Nor will it really help you to save time because it is unlikely to be done well and in the end you may have to do it yourself anyway. It is better to see delegation as an opportunity for staff development, giving other people more challenging and worthwhile tasks which will save you considerably more time than delegating boring and repetitious ones.

One of the reasons managers don't delegate effectively is because they are perfectionists and expect their staff to achieve unnecessarily high standards as the two examples below illustrate.

'I used to spend several hours doing unnecessary clerical work although I have a production clerk who is supposed to do it. I realized that the reason I was doing it myself was because I expected the production clerk to achieve a perfect result every time. When I thought about it, a satisfactory result would have been good enough and the occasional failure wouldn't have been a disaster. By changing my thinking, I was able to delegate more tasks to the clerk and use my own time more effectively.'

'I find it difficult to delegate, mainly because I don't want my staff to feel I delegate too much. I feel this could be seen as a weakness and also I do not trust them to do the job as well as I do. This means when I do delegate, I am constantly checking on them to ensure the work is up to standard - my standard. At my appraisal, my manager discussed this failure of mine to delegate and suggested I saw it as helping my staff to understand their jobs better. Now I delegate the daily completion of work figures and the production of a weekly plan to my team and it is amazing to see how much better they understand how well – or poorly – they are performing.'

PLANNING YOUR WORKLOAD

Overwork and work-related stress are two of the major problems faced by today's managers, while the work–life balance is an issue which has steadily risen up managers' agendas in recent years.

Japan's biggest advertising agency has been forced to pay the equivalent of £780,000 to the family of a man who committed suicide after working for 17 months without a day off. Ichiro Oshima often worked late – at times until dawn – with only two or three hours sleep before returning to his desk by 9 a.m. Death from overwork, or 'karoshi', has long been a sensitive issue in Japan. Workaholic tendencies are widespread because of pressures to be loyal to the corporate 'family'.

We touched on workload planning in relation to setting priorities and, of course, it is also related to effective delegation. Managers often spend considerable time in planning and allocating the work of their staff, and very little on organizing their own workload.

Rosemary Stewart (1982) has developed a way of looking at a manager's job in terms of its demands and constraints and the degree of choice, or control, which the individual can exercise.

'Demands', according to Stewart, are tasks you must do. Demands can come from your superiors and your peers, from people outside the organization in the form of requests for information or action, from the system in the form of reports or budgets you are required to submit, from your staff who may need guidance or appraisal and, finally from yourself – the work you feel you must do because of your personal standards or habits. Some of these demands may be able to be reduced – others cannot.

'Constraints' limit what you can do. These may include resource limitations, legal regulations, union agreements, technological or physical limitations, organizational policies and procedures and people's attitudes towards you, and expectations about your role as a manager. Such limitations are often difficult to change.

The area of 'choice' shown in Figure 2.1 is the extent to which the manager can choose what is done (or not done) and how it is done; there are also usually elements of choice in when the work is done, by whom (delegation) and to what standard.

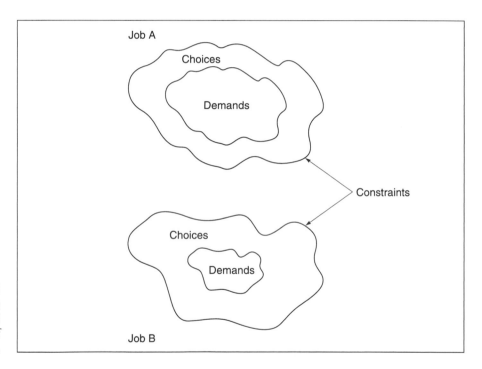

Figure 2.1
Looking at the demands and constraints of managers' jobs.

In Figure 2.1, Job A has heavy demands and between these demands and the constraints within which it is performed, there is little area for choice. Job B, on the other hand, leaves the manager with considerable area of choice between the demands of the job and the constraints within which it is performed. The manager who holds Job A really needs to look at the demands of the job; there are too many of them, some of which may be unrealistic. Maybe he or she needs more staff so that some of the demands can be passed on to others; or perhaps a discussion with the line manager might reduce some of the demands which are being imposed from above.

Investigate

> Try describing your job in terms of demands, constraints and choice. If the demands made on you are too heavy, how might these be reduced? Using your area of choice, can you plan your workload more effectively?

Chapter 9 deals with stress as a challenge for managers, mainly in the context of employee stress, but it is very important for managers to appreciate that they too are as susceptible to stress, and indeed arguably even more so, than their subordinates. A survey of 4,600 Barclays' Bank managers revealed that a quarter have received medical treatment for stress-related illnesses in the previous five years. Nearly half the managers felt insecure in their jobs and 19 per cent worked up to, and sometimes over, 25 hours a week overtime. Barclays has contracted a counselling service to cope with employees' problems.

A part of managing your workload is achieving an appropriate work–life balance, and this is far from easy for many managers. British workers have a notoriously high workweek compared to their European counterparts, and managers work amongst the longest hours within the workforce. Obviously a key to the work–life balance is consideration of and time spent with your family, but a balance is not just about this. It is very desirable to have interests outside work, whether these are hobbies, sport, or membership of organizations; apart from anything else, think of the people you know who have an unfulfilled retirement because they have no interests and often no good reason for living. And a further dimension is health; you need to take time out to have some level of exercise if you are not to allow your health to degenerate.

A 2000 survey by the Institute of Management indicated that the work–life balance is seen as a significant challenge for managers, rating higher than issues such as acquiring needed skills, financial/budget constraints, and increased competitive activity. In an earlier IM survey in 1997, almost two-thirds of both male and female managers felt that work and home life are equally important; interestingly enough, a higher percentage of women (22%) than men (14%) felt that work was more or much more important.

MAKING DECISIONS

There are, according to the American social scientist, Herbert Simon, two main kinds of decisions which anyone is called upon to make. There are 'programmed' decisions which can be made for problems or events which have occurred before, such as processing a customer's order, determining an employee's holiday entitlement or carrying out any routine job. And there are 'non-programmed' decisions which have to be made where there is no cut-and-dried method for handling the problem, either because it has not occurred before or because it is particularly difficult or important. To help with the uncertainties of non-programmed decision-making, Simon (1960) developed a model of rational thinking which involved three stages – Intelligence, Design and Choice (Figure 2.2).

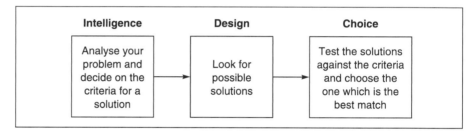

Figure 2.2
A rational decision-making model

The three stages could be broken down into a series of smaller steps. At the Intelligence stage, the problem needs to be defined and clarified so that everyone is clear about what the problem actually is. Once the problem has been defined, then criteria need to be drawn up so that any solution can be evaluated against these. In the Design stage, possible solutions should be generated and, in the Choice stage, these possible solutions should be evaluated against the criteria and the best option selected.

Investigate

Think about a problem you have at work and which you have to address. Try applying the rational decision-making model to this problem.

ACTIVE LISTENING

Part of your job as a manager is likely to involve listening to people – listening to their problems, successes and worries, their reports on progress, their reasons for not progressing, their grievances and ideas. Listening is a skill and 'active listening' is a particular skill; it is all too easy to listen without hearing what is being said, which is why this section is titled 'active listening'.

✗ Active listening involves more than passively absorbing what is being said; it entails trying to understand what the speaker is saying and helping them to clarify what they mean for both of you – getting 'inside' the speaker and suspending your own judgement. One of the aims of active listening is to encourage the speaker to come up with their own solution, not to offer advice.

Another very important part of active listening is in its contribution to your knowledge of what is happening in your unit, and being an effective manager means knowing what is happening around you. It is often not what is said that is important, but how it is said. Unless you can understand the nuances of what people are trying to tell you, you may miss the reality of the situation. Gossip, jokes, and casual comments are part of the key to understanding the informal dynamics of your unit, and indeed the wider organization.

The skills of active listening take time to acquire and need a lot of practice. As a manager, you have many opportunities for practice. Next time someone comes into your office with a problem, try the following:

- Either give them your full attention at that moment or arrange a time when you can give them all your attention.
- Don't take the words at face value; encourage the person to expand on what they are saying.
- Watch the non-verbal communication; is the person more or less worried than he or she appears – are there signs outside the words themselves which indicate anything?
- Check your understanding of what is being said; reflect in your own words what the speaker seems to be saying – perhaps you have misunderstood them.
- Try to convey 'I respect you as a person and feel you are worth listening to' through all your words and actions.
- Encourage the person to try to articulate possible solutions to the problem.

COMMUNICATING

Managers need to communicate and communication is a two-way process, otherwise it might as well be called 'munication' according to Derek Rowntree (1988). Depending on the type of communication, it can involve giving, receiving or seeking information. Even the casual greeting, 'Hallo, how are you?', is, effectively, seeking information about the other person's state of health. The common reply, 'Fine – how about you?', is both giving and seeking information on the speaker's part while the listener is receiving information.

We communicate with a wide range of people in our working lives as Figure 2.3 shows, and this can be called our 'communication network'.

Investigate

> Have a go at drawing up your own communication network. You can make this more complex and realistic by drawing communication links between others on the network – for example, in Figure 2.3, the restaurant owner would probably communicate with other owners. Now make a list of the different ways in which you communicate with other people.

We can categorize the ways in which we communicate into the spoken word and the written word, although this neglects communicating pictorially or graphically. We can also take into account the non-verbal aspects of communicating.

Communicating through the spoken word includes face-to-face communication between individuals and groups, presentations and speeches, telephone converzations and videoconferencing. Written communication can be on paper in the form of letters, memos, reports, newsletters, articles, books and so on and via electronic means such as electronic mail, computer-mediated conferencing and the Internet. Non-verbal communication can include the tone of voice, accent, facial expression, gestures, body language and personal choice of clothes, decoration, lifestyle etc.

But communication is not a simple process and too often people can misunderstand what others have said or written. It is not just what you communicate but how you do it. The use of complex, long-winded language can create problems in understanding as can using an inappropriate method of communicating. For example, complicated directions are usually communicated more effectively through a map than by word of mouth – providing the map is accurate! Jargon can cause difficulties for people who are not familiar with

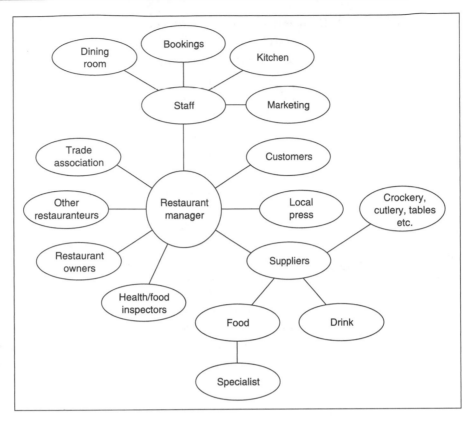

Figure 2.3
A restaurant
manager's
communication
network

it, as can acronyms. 'Take the hot batch down to TCR right away' could be incomprehensible to anyone not familiar with the terms and initials.

✳Communication is also about what you are trying to achieve. Managers usually have three objectives in communicating: getting employees to understand and accept what the manager proposes should be done; obtaining the commitment of the employees to these proposals; and to help the employees to appreciate the contribution that they will be making to the success of the proposals and how this will benefit them. It follows that communicating is more than merely telling people something but should also include a capacity for foreseeing and appreciating their likely response. What you say therefore requires thinking through before you say it. A golden rule in communicating effectively is to continually reflect back on what has been said, checking that your understanding matches that of the speaker, and to check, when you are speaking, that the listener shares your understanding of what you have said.

Communicating is also about informing people about issues that they might reasonably expect to know about. There is a view that 'knowledge is power' and that people should be told things strictly on a need-to-know basis; their special knowledge, in some managers' opinion, is how they emphasize the distinction in status between them and their subordinates. This is not a wise position to take, although there will be some knowledge that cannot be shared. People will only feel part of a team and appreciated if they are kept informed about developments. Briefings, newsletters, or other means of informing people should also provide some means by which they can also express opinions. Most people will not do so, but will nevertheless welcome the opportunity.

COUNSELLING

> Somebody called it 'corridor converzations' – a slight exaggeration, but it does underline the fact that a lot of good counselling and helping is done in passing, does not need to take long, does not have to be in a formal setting and does not require a degree to do it. (Reddy, 1987)

Counselling is used rather loosely as a term when, often, it means advising. Organizations use counselling in a variety of ways, for example career counselling, redundancy counselling and the kinds of counselling associated with appraisal systems and disciplinary procedures. It is used, mainly, to help employees solve their own problems or make their own decisions. Problems that need professional help, such as alcohol or drug abuse, depression and serious personal and domestic problems, should always be referred to a specialist who is trained to give advice and help in these and other matters. It is potentially dangerous and damaging for an untrained person to attempt to intervene in such cases.

Reddy, who has considerable experience of training and supervising counsellors, considers that effective counsellors need to be tolerant, have knowledge of themselves, be discreet and have an interest in and a liking for people (Reddy, 1987). Too often, people responsible for formal or informal counselling at work have no training and are lacking in some or all of the above qualities; they 'counsel' because it is part of their job.

It is often during the annual appraisal or performance review that counselling becomes a major part of the manager's job, particularly if you have to appraise someone who has been performing badly. This is the time when you have to get to the heart of what is causing inadequate performance – and the person being appraised may be reluctant to tell you or be unaware of the cause themselves.

The first essential is to define the problem between yourself and the other person and ensure that you both understand what it is. This involves the skills of 'active listening' we discussed earlier. For example, an employee who is not performing up to standard tells you emphatically that it is the fault of the new machine, the new process or a new member of staff – the 'it's not my fault' syndrome. By careful and sensitive probing, you discover that the fault lies in lack of training or the employee's fear that someone else will take over their job. The next stage in counselling is to get the employee to recognize this while you both accept that it is not necessarily 'their fault'.

Once the problem has been redefined in a way which satisfies you both – and this is not always possible – you need to be able to provide a solution which is mutually acceptable. This might involve offering training or support of some kind; it might involve ensuring that the person receives regular feedback on their performance, which reassures them that they are doing the job well or indicates ways in which they might improve their performance.

Throughout all this, you need to gain the trust of the other person. He or she needs to be sure that you have their interests at heart and that you are not likely to use the information you now have about them to their detriment. As a manager, you represent the organization when you are counselling staff; sometimes the organization is at fault, by not providing adequate training, for example, or by decreasing an individual's job satisfaction. You, and the organization, have then to take responsibility for contributing to the individual's problem.

Investigate

In what ways does your organization expect you to formally counsel your staff? Does it provide adequate resources (e.g. training) for this purpose and does it accept responsibility for contributing to problems when this occurs?

In the same way as different problems need different solutions, different situations at work are likely to require different styles of counselling. And individuals have their own preferences for adopting particular styles:

- The client-centred style depends on the counsellor 'reflecting' back to the other person – the client – the key issues and encouraging the client to reach their own solution.
- The supportive style relies on the counsellor being able to empathize with the client, minimizing feelings of isolation, guilt or weakness in the latter.
- The interpretive style is more realistic than the supportive style since it recognizes that the counsellor cannot always know what the other person is feeling. Instead of saying 'I know how you are feeling ...', the counsellor using this kind of style would be more likely to say 'Is this how you are feeling – have I got it right?'
- The probing style is more appropriate for fact-finding, but there are often times when counsellors need to check facts and also to probe where they feel they are not hearing the whole story.
- The evaluative style is close to problem-solving and involves offering advice. It is probably the least successful.

Investigate   Which of the above counselling styles holds most attraction for you? Can you think of times when it would not be appropriate?

DEVELOPING YOURSELF

What have you done recently to increase your competence as a manager? Like all too many others, you might well reply:

- 'I was sent on the company's three-day leadership course last May' or
- 'We have an in-service training course on selection interviewing – I went on that' or
- 'I'm thinking about going on a course on managing time'.

Most managers who work in organizations without a stated management development policy manage to get some training in a rather piecemeal way; perhaps they hear of a course, or there is a note about one in the company newsletter or on the notice board. 'That looks interesting ...' they say to themselves, and put their names down for it. Some managers are more proactive and seek out training before trying to persuade their employers to pay for them; others are forced to fund their own training.

Investigate

Which category of manager are you, reactive, or proactive, or even someone who takes no interest in development at all? Ask yourself what you have done in the past and consider whether this is good enough for the future.

It is not possible to improve the performance of those who work under you without developing them, and in turn that cannot be effective without recognizing your own need for development. In a context of rapid change, where the shelf-life of knowledge is between two and ten years, you will rapidly become out of date without development. Your career needs to be managed actively, not just left to develop by chance or at the behest of an employer. It involves being able to look backwards as well as forwards, and to be able to learn from what has happened to date. The concept of career is becoming more diffuse, and very few managers can now expect a job for life. You need to ask yourself what your objectives are, and to identify your career 'anchors' which reflect your values and priorities. Schein (1978) identified eight different categories of career anchor:

- Technical/functional where the anchor is achieving specific skills.
- Entrepreneurial where the anchor is developing a business.
- General managerial competence, where the anchor is general management.
- Service/dedication, where the anchor is commitment to a moral goal.
- Autonomy/independence, where the anchor is being your own master, even in employment.
- Pure challenge, where the anchor is being challenged by a job.
- Security/stability, where the anchor is a safe and stable job.
- Lifestyle, where the anchor is the balance of external interests with the career.

Good self-development requires good, i.e. critical, self-awareness, it requires an ability to carry out a training needs analysis on yourself, and it requires the commitment to carry it through. Your employer will doubtless have a training programme, but these differ considerably. It is important to be able to take the initiative yourself, and in all probability go beyond the range of training offered to relate to your own wider career needs. A key issue is learning how to learn; it is arguable that in taking a qualification the key is not the knowledge obtained but developing the ability to learn and apply the learning to the job. Your career is the most important aspect of your working life; be prepared to invest in it. Moreover self-development is on-going and lifelong, as the term Continuing Professional Development (CPD) implies. Kotter (1995), in his review of the careers of the class of 1974 at Harvard Business School, argued that the ability to go on learning was one of the two most important factors in career success. There are many types of self-development; taking a qualification is one, attending a seminar about new ideas is another, but even more important is developing the ability to learn from experience, by reflecting on the lessons of what has happened and drawing conclusions from them as to how best to move forward. What every manager needs is a Personal Development Plan (PDP).

Planning your own career and self-development involves acquiring information about jobs inside your own organization and possibilities outside it. It involves systematically assessing your own strengths and weaknesses. It means matching your strengths to the requirements of other jobs and reducing your weaknesses through training and skill acquisition. It requires a lot of self-investigation, complete honesty, and determination.

Investigate

Try to get hold of the job description of a post which you aspire to in your organization. With complete honesty, evaluate your personal strengths and weaknesses against the requirements of the job. Where possible, get someone else at work who knows you well to evaluate these for you. What do you need to do next?

MANAGING YOUR MANAGER

Like most books on management, this one offers you plenty of advice on managing your staff; unlike most books on management, it also offers you some ideas at this point on managing your boss – managing the manager who manages you.

As you saw earlier, your superiors – and, in most cases, your line manager – will be one of those who makes demands on you in your job. Your line manager will be the person responsible for appraising you and discussing your performance with you. He or she is likely to be asked for a reference if you are seeking promotion or a new job and can represent your interests and those of your team to senior management. It is very much in your interests to have a good working relationship with this person!

Unfortunately, you can rarely choose your line manager and there are 'bad' bosses as well as 'good' ones. A good line manager respects his or her staff, acknowledges their strengths and helps them to overcome their weaknesses. He or she takes your part in inter-departmental negotiations, supports you, deals with you fairly and honestly, delegates and communicates effectively and gives you opportunities to be involved in decision-making, particularly when the decisions affect you and your area of responsibility.

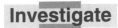

Investigate

How would you rate your lin̲_____i̲n̲st the description in the above paragraph?
How would you rate your̲

Managing your relations̲
or her expectations of̲
work for a 'problem'̲
in you, sees you as̲
you what is happe̲
that you should̲
suggestions for̲
are a small m̲

are recorded in

to find out if they

Don't:
■
■
■

_____ manager's manager;
_____ with your colleagues
_____

experiencing problems;

35

- take any instances of sexual or racial discrimination or harassment to a higher authority in the organization;
- consider lodging a formal complaint;
- consider leaving the job.

Summary

In this chapter we have asked you to consider a range of ways in which you can manage yourself more effectively and, thus, become a more effective manager of people. Reading about ways to manage your time and your workload, communicate, make decisions and delegate is not likely to increase your managerial effectiveness; this can only happen when you put some of the ideas into practice in your own work situation.

You might like to go over some of the Investigations again in those areas in which you feel you are weak to see if they give you any ideas about how to improve and become more effective.

Activities

1 At the end of each working day, allow yourself ten minutes in which to list and prioritize the tasks for the next day. Allocate the boring and difficult tasks to the first hour of the next day – and tackle them then.
2 How could you reduce your workload and use your time more productively by delegating some of it to your subordinates?
3 Think about your current work–life balance. How does it fit with what you and your family want?

   List the times you are required to counsel staff on a formal
   informal basis every week. How could you improve your
   lling skills?

CHAPTER 3

Recruiting the right people

INTRODUCTION

This chapter is concerned with defining future staff requirements and determining the best way of recruiting quality people, particularly in your own area of responsibility although these should, ideally, be set in a context of overall organizational personnel requirements. This and the next chapter, dealing with selection and induction, are in some respects the most important in the book. By far the biggest component of the successful management of people is having the right people to pursue the organization's objectives. This means not only people who can do their own job in a technical sense, but who can also appreciate other people's jobs and work with them in a group or team towards wider objectives. And it is much more difficult for you as a manager to manage people who perhaps should not have been there in the first place. Not only is there an element of inefficiency and possible disruption built in from the start, but the costs of remedying the situation in terms of the ultimate sanction of sacking someone can be very expensive both in financial and emotional terms. In this chapter, we will be examining the following topics:

- Determining human resource requirements.
- Job analysis.
- Job descriptions.
- Employee specification.
- Methods of recruiting candidates.
- Further information for candidates.
- The application format.

DETERMINING HUMAN RESOURCE REQUIREMENTS

In Chapter 1, you looked at some of the recent trends in organizations and in skill needs. These should have given you some idea of the kinds of people organizations need to develop or recruit in the twenty-first century.

There will be a need for people who can operate in the rest of Europe; for managers familiar with the use of information technology; for people who understand the environment in which the organization operates; for people who are willing and able to acquire new skills and knowledge; for people able to make decisions as the context and environment change. Organizations and their managers will need to be involved in human resource auditing and planning to determine their future needs.

Planning for the future is no longer easy as the future becomes less predictable and change more rapid. You can no longer afford to recruit staff on job descriptions that have been around for years; you are going to need people who can be flexible, adaptable and respond to new challenges. This means, too, that you should look beyond your normal sources of staff since these may no longer be appropriate for your needs.

You will also need to be aware of current and new legislation governing the recruitment of people in a wider European labour market; in particular, you need to avoid discrimination on the grounds of gender, race or disability. These regulatory issues are covered in Chapter 10.

Human resource planning has been around for more than a quarter of a century. Initially, it was based on complex models which were based on operations research and were incomprehensible to anyone but mathematicians. These models were intended to forecast long-term trends but they failed to operate successfully in attempts to reduce unemployment or to anticipate skill shortages. The pace of change outran the adequacy of this means of planning for the future.

During the 1970s, human resource accounting became popular, i.e. applying principles of financial accounting to human resources. However, human resources, unlike fixed assets, tend to appreciate with experience rather than depreciate with age and this appreciation is very difficult to estimate in financial terms (Pearson, 1991). In the mid-1980s, scenario planning came into favour. This involved the design of models of best and worst scenarios as far as organizational human resource needs were concerned and could be computerized to produce 'what if' scenarios. What if . . . there is another major UK or European recession? What if . . . new technology overtakes the skills of current staff? It is possible, given the reluctance of organizations to change, that your own organization uses one or other of these methods despite their failure to predict human resource needs with any accuracy.

The first stage in the recruitment process is therefore to determine human resource needs now and in the future. Any strategic plan for the future of an organization needs to be expressed not only in terms of what the organization expects to achieve, but also the ways in which these achievements can be fulfilled. This includes the numbers and type of staff the organization is likely to need in both the short-term and long-term future. But while doing this, it is desirable also to bear in mind the need for a policy on retention; it is much cheaper to keep people than it is to recruit them.

Investigate

What methods does your organization use to plan for future staffing levels? Does it provide a clear indication of the type and numbers of staff the organization will need in the future? Does it have a policy for retention of the existing staff?

JOB ANALYSIS: AUDITING EXISTING HUMAN RESOURCES

The first stage in developing a plan for your area of responsibility involves analysing the skills and knowledge already available to you amongst the people already working for you – sometimes called a Human Resource Audit. In this way, you can begin to identify skill deficiencies and plan to remedy these deficiencies through recruitment.

Recruiting staff for a job which already exists needs to take into account ways in which that job may change in the future. But are you sure that you know what the job entails at the moment? Looking at an existing job description may be misleading since it is likely, if the jobholder has been in the post for some time, that the job has already changed within that period.

Let us assume that a member of your staff has handed in his/her notice and you have a vacancy to fill. How do you find out what the job really entails? We have already said that existing job descriptions can be unreliable; so, too, can be the description of the job by the present jobholder. Try analysing your own job and see how difficult it is, so the jobholder's description is only of value if it is supported by other evidence.

Your objectives in carrying out this exercise are fourfold.

First, what is the purpose of the job? Is it necessary? Is it fulfilling its purpose?

Second, could the job be combined with other jobs to make it more fulfilling or could some parts of it be reallocated to make better use of the skills of other people in the department?

Third, could a full-time job be shared between two people working part-time? Could all or part of the job be carried out in the jobholder's home? Could more flexible working hours be introduced? This would enable you to widen your recruitment to include people who, for a variety of reasons, could not undertake either a full-time job or travel to and from home.

Fourth, what have I learned about the job from analysing it?

When you have gone through these processes, and you are satisfied that you have enough information about the job, and that this information is clear and unambiguous, you are almost ready to move on to write, or rewrite, a job description. But, bearing in mind the changing environment in which we all work, you also need to consider whether the job as you have analysed it is likely to stay the same or to change in the foreseeable future. Will the next jobholder require different skills if the job is to change or grow? For example, is your organization planning to move into markets outside the UK and are you likely to need people who can speak languages other than English or who are willing to be mobile?

Another dimension relates to patterns of work. A number of companies have taken positive action to recruit and retain working mothers. Sainsbury, Boots and B&Q among others offer jobs where working hours are confined to school terms. ICI have improved their maternity pay and designed working hours which fit in with school hours and holidays; as a result, the number of women managers working for the company has increased. BhS has also adopted a system of flexible working hours. They offer two types of contract, one related to working during school terms only and another for employees who want to specify their own hours and are prepared to work on a standby basis.

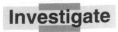 **Investigate**

What patterns of work does your employer use? Does your organization operate any jobshare schemes, opportunities for homeworking or flexitime? If not, could these be introduced?

JOB DESCRIPTIONS

A good job description is a vital part of recruitment. ACAS, the Advisory, Conciliation and Arbitration Service, suggests that a job description should be drawn up under the following headings.

1 The title of the job

Most jobs have a title such as Project Manager, Filing Clerk, Supervisor and so on. However, is the old job title still valid after your analysis or does it need to be changed to reflect the changed nature of the job? Examine the current job title critically; does it really describe the job? And does it imply any descriptive discrimination in terms of race, gender or disability, e.g. salesman?

2 The main purpose of the job

Your job analysis should have teased this out and you should aim to describe the purpose of the job in one sentence. For example:

> **Job Title**
> Administrative Secretary
> **Main purpose of the job**
> Supervising the work of secretarial and clerical
> staff in the department in order to provide high-
> quality secretarial support to the senior
> management team.

3 The main tasks of the job

Here, again, the job analysis should have identified these but you need to make them as clear as possible. Use verbs such as 'writing ...', 'filing ...', 'designing ...', 'planning ...' etc. which actively describe what the job involves. Avoid vague terms such as 'in charge of ...'.

4 The scope of the job

You have already stated the main tasks of the job but this gives little indication of how important the job is. In this section you need to give an idea of, for example, the number of people for whom the job-holder would be responsible or the budget he/she would control or the value of the equipment or materials handled, and how the job itself relates to the overall work of the department or organization.

EMPLOYEE SPECIFICATION – ALSO KNOWN AS PERSON SPECIFICATION

Once you have completed a satisfactory job description, you should draw up a description of the type of person you feel would best per-form the job. This should be done under four main headings and each heading should be subdivided into 'essential' and 'desirable' qualities in the person you are seeking. Those qualities which are categorized as 'essential' are necessary to adequate performance of the job; with-out them, the job could not be performed either effectively or effi-ciently. 'Desirable' qualities should be seen as additional assets which would enhance effective performance of the job.

Skills

Your employee specification should focus on qualities which the potential jobholder should already possess, or be capable of acquiring through experience or training in order to perform the job effec-tively. Your job analysis and job description should have identified these for you and you should include any skills which might be neces-sary for performance of the job if and when it changes in the future. Some manual skill requirements could be seen to discriminate against disabled people; in fact, the Disablement Advisory Service can pro-vide equipment which can enable disabled people to perform most jobs.

The voluntary organization, Action for Blind People aims to encourage employers to increase the number of visually impaired people in work. There is a need to dispel some of the myths about the employment of blind or partially-sighted people since many employers believe that it will cost them more to provide equipment or that they are likely to be absent from the workplace more often than sighted employees. For this purpose, Action for Blind People provides an employer information pack, backed up by other services which they provide on a voluntary basis.

Knowledge

This may be technical, professional, administrative or organizational but it must be relevant to the effective performance of the job. Some highly specialized knowledge may be gained through provision for training in the job rather than be expected in applicants.

Experience

The amount of relevant experience, and the level, should be carefully assessed in relation to the requirements of the job itself. Some specifications discriminate unfairly against some groups of people. For example, if you felt current experience was essential, this would discriminate against women returners; you should ask yourself if this was not, in fact, a 'desirable' quality or, indeed, really necessary at all.

Attitudes

This subheading refers to behavioural qualities such as the ability to work in a team or to take initiative or work without supervision. Often, this is the hardest area of the employee specification against which to measure applicants and your selection procedure will need to be designed to determine whether or not candidates actually have the attitudes you consider important.

Everything you include in the employee specification should relate closely to your job description and should be capable of being described and measured so that you are able to make an informed and accurate decision about the best candidate for the job.

METHODS OF RECRUITING CANDIDATES

Internal recruitment

First of all, you have to decide whether you need to recruit candidates from outside the organization to take over a vacant job. Many organizations have a policy to give preference to internal candidates, at least in certain circumstances, such as where there are likely to be appropriate skills elsewhere. Operating an internal labour market policy also helps to cut the cost of recruitment both directly, as in not having to pay for advertisements, and indirectly, in that the candidates will have been socialized in the values and ways of working of the organization. If you have carried out an audit of the people in your area of responsibility, you should have a good idea of the skills, knowledge, experience and attitudes of your existing staff and it may make more sense to promote someone internally or to move someone sideways as part of their career development.

Job advertisements

By far the most common method of external recruitment is through advertisements; it is also the method most fraught with misunderstanding, misinterpretation and potential lawbreaking, and it can also be an expensive operation, costing several thousands of pounds for prominent advertisements in the national newspapers. A key decision is what the most appropriate newspaper or magazine is; most now have special sections to appeal to particular types of people, such as education on Tuesdays, computing on Wednesdays, and media on Thursdays. Organizations that operate equal opportunities policies ensure that recruitment advertisements are not just placed in traditional white, middle-class newspapers and journals but in media which are read by people from different ethnic and religious backgrounds; they also take positive action to encourage the employment of people from all minority groups.

There has been considerable research into how people react to advertisements for jobs, both published and unpublished (Schofield, 1992). The main findings relevant to this chapter are:

- that readers scanning recruitment pages in newspapers and journals spend, on average, just one and a half seconds on each advertisement;
- that heavy black borders around advertisements are a barrier to scanning and fewer people read the advertisement inside;
- that the most important factor people look for in a job is interesting work, followed by prospects of promotion, salary, security, personal involvement with the job and education/ training opportunities;

■ that, where an individual is actually named in an advertisement as the person to whom job applications should be sent, there is a significantly higher response than if only a job title or department is given.

As already pointed out, one of the criteria of recruitment is that it is cost-effective. Poor job advertisements waste time and money since they attract candidates who are unsuitable for the job; good advertisements are specifically designed to attract candidates who can and want to do the job effectively. As well as the Schofield review noted above, Iles (2001) has noted that 'applicants appear to respond well to recruiters who are seen as competent, informed, credible, and impersonally skilled. Especially at the early stages of recruitment, these positive impressions of recruiters seem to influence applicants' willingness to take up job offers'.

Only a little thought is needed to convince us that the perfect advertisement would attract only one reply and that from the right person. Let us begin with an extreme example:

Wanted: Acrobat capable of crossing a slack wire 200 feet above a raging furnace. Twice nightly, three times on Saturday. Salary offered £25 per week. No pension and no compenzation in the event of injury. Apply in person at Wildcat Circus between the hours of 9 a.m. and 10 a.m.

The wording of this may not be perfect but the aim should be so to balance the inducement in salary against the possible risks involved that only a single applicant will appear. It is needless to ask for details of qualifications and experience. No one unskilled on the slack wire would find the offer attractive. It is needless to insist that candidates should be physically fit, sober and free from fits of dizziness. They know that. It is just as needless to stipulate that those nervous of heights need not apply. They won't. The skill of the advertiser consists in adjusting the salary to the danger. An offer of £1,000 per week might produce a dozen applicants. An offer of £15 might produce none. Somewhere between those two figures lies the exact sum to specify the minimum figure to attract anyone actually capable of doing the job. If there is more than one applicant, the figure has been placed a trifle too high. (Parkinson, 1986)

Investigate

Try to get hold of a recruitment advertisement your organization has used recently. In light of what you have just read, how effective is it likely to be?

Traditional sources of recruits

In the past, and to a considerable extent still today, organizations have had links with educational institutions, such as schools, colleges and universities, which have been a main source of job applicants. These links might go so far as to a particular teacher who would recommend likely students. Some companies spend a lot of money in producing glossy brochures and undertaking a 'milk round' to search for the best graduates. Alternatively, there are the state-operated employment exchanges or job centres – the title seems to change quite frequently, where unemployed people 'sign up' and look for job opportunities.

The Internet

However, the advent of the Internet has made an impact in this area, and is likely to become of increasing importance. Major companies are starting to recruit employees on the Internet. Employers provide details of jobs which potential candidates can access, completing a standardized CV which they submit online. The advantage for employers is in the very low cost and the speed with which they can get a job vacancy advertised on the Internet which can be accessed by people outside the UK as well as inside. Many professional and managerial jobs are now advertised on the Internet, but there are still many jobs where prospective applicants are unlikely to use the Internet as a source of job opportunities, and even in the managerial area it would probably not be sensible to make it the only mode of attracting applicants.

> Monster.com looks likely to become the world's largest on-line recruiter, following a $119m (£86m) bid for its pan-European rival Jobline.

Recruitment agencies

There are now many well-known companies which specialize in providing staff, usually at a white collar level, reflecting the increasing numbers of organizations which have externalized their recruitment activities. However, they can be quite expensive, charging a percentage of the first year's salary. Within the same category and often the same companies are those which provide temporary or contract staff.

Some major companies, such as IBM, now prefer to have a high proportion of their staff on a contractual basis rather than as permanent employees, and this approach is spreading in the technical areas such as computing and engineering.

Headhunters

Headhunters, or as they normally prefer to call themselves, recruitment consultants, are only used for very specific and usually very high-level recruitment. They normally produce a short-list after trawling likely applicants and sometimes carrying out a preliminary interview. Their advantage is that they can approach individuals who are unlikely to be reading advertisements, and who may have no immediate intention of leaving their existing employer. Although obviously not cheap, they can be cost effective if they find the right person.

Previous applicants

A further source of recruits can be built up using a computer database of unsuccessful candidates. Computerized recruitment systems enable employers to cultivate large databases of applicants which become the first source turned to as vacancies arise. Running a single advertisement may elicit 200 responses. If one candidate is hired, this leaves a resource of 199 applications that, without a recruitment system, would be wasted at a cost to the company of approximately £50 per capita.

> Key data, such as skills, educational qualifications, previous employers and experience, all with relevant dates, is extracted from applications. The computer then reorganizes this information into a standard summary and compares it with every vacancy within the organization, flagging up any matches. Should no matches occur, the system retains the information and compares it with every new opening that subsequently arises in the organization. (Theaker, 1995)

There are, of course, disadvantages to this type of systemization of recruitment. Applicants on the database may no longer be free to take up employment or they may have no interest in a job for which they have not specifically applied. Similarly, managers may be reluctant to hire someone who has not applied for a particular post.

Investigate   Which sources of recruits does your organization use? Should you be thinking about widening the recruitment net by investigating other sources?

The basic criteria for methods of recruitment are that they should be cost-effective and that there is no hint of discrimination on sex, race or disability grounds. Recently, there has been an ongoing debate about discrimination on the grounds of age – or 'ageism'. It is not illegal (at the time of writing) to put age limits in recruitment advertisements, but it is discriminatory and bad practice. The Institute of Personnel and Development put the following statement in its journal in January 1996 shortly before a private member's bill in the House of Commons failed to make the practice illegal.

'From this, our first issue of 1996, we will no longer accept any recruitment advertisement for publication that excludes some applicants purely on the grounds of their age. We are unwilling to play any part in prolonging misguided attitudes and patterns of behaviour among a minority of employers and advertising agencies, based on faulty assumptions and outdated personnel and recruitment practice.' (*People Management*, January 1996)

In today's uncertain employment climate, discrimination on the grounds of age is a very real fear for many people made redundant in mid-career. One 48-year-old job candidate took a positive approach in his application for employment by writing 'Think of me as an 18-year-old with 30 years' experience.'

FURTHER INFORMATION FOR CANDIDATES

Potential employees will also want to know more about the job than can be put in an advertisement or most other approaches to recruitment. Prospective applicants should thus be encouraged to request additional information – usually referred to as 'further particulars'. For some types of job, the prospective applicants might be encouraged to talk to a key person, either in the personnel department or the manager who will be in charge of them; this can either be done in person or on the phone.

In the whole approach to recruitment, the way in which the process is described can be important on being either welcoming or off-putting. A frequently used example of a poorly worded advertisement is:

'Further particulars may be obtained on application to the Personnel Officer to whom typewritten curriculum vitae (six copies) with the names and addresses of two referees should be sent by ...'

This may be organizational practice, but is it really necessary? It is certainly discouraging and it says something about an organization which might put good candidates off. A better, applicant-friendly alternative is:

'For an information pack, including details of how to apply, please telephone Mary Adams on ...'

The further information for job candidates can be drawn mainly from the job description and employee specification. It should also include information about the organization as a whole. The Information Pack should 'sell' your organization to potential candidates and should contain:

- essential and realistic details of the job, its place in the organization, and the potential terms and conditions of employment, including a description of the potential psychological contract;
- information about the organization such as an Annual Report (if there is one) and some indication of its size, achievements and future plans;
- information about the essential and desirable qualities required for the post, drawn from your employee specification;
- the name and telephone number of someone in the organization (in agreement with that person) whom candidates can contact if they want to ask questions about the job or find out more from someone 'on the ground';

■ information about how the selection process will be carried out.

The British Ceramic Confederation has produced a brochure designed to recruit young people into the industry. It gives an overview of the ceramics industry and the kinds of career opportunities it offers in areas such as production, sales and marketing. The brochure includes studies of young people who have entered the industry from a range of backgrounds and is accompanied by a video.

Investigate

Does your organization send out an Information Pack or comprehensive information to job applicants?

THE APPLICATION FORMAT

You are also going to have to consider in what form you want applications to be made. Your organization may have a standard application form which was designed many years ago and is now unsuitable for its purpose – have a look at it and decide whether it meets your needs or whether it needs to be adapted or redesigned. Any application form should be designed to give the maximum information about the candidate which is relevant to the requirements of the job. This can include relevant educational, technical and/or professional qualifications essential for performance of the job, previous job history and relevant experience and any special requirements such as the ability to speak a particular language or the need to hold a current driving licence if these are necessary to the performance of the job. The application form should not require details of marital status or dependants, nationality or disabilities; it should use the term 'forename' and not 'Christian name'.

You may also ask for a Curriculum Vitae (CV) or a letter of application instead of, or in addition to, a completed application form: look at the requirements of the job and decide which form(s) of application would be most useful when it comes to making an initial selection.

Finally, you have to ensure that in no way does your advertisement contravene the law governing discrimination in recruitment advertising; it should not suggest that the job is open only to persons of one sex, race, religion or particular marital status, with some very limited exceptions where there is a genuine occupational need for a certain type of person. If it does discriminate, a complaint may be lodged with the Equal Opportunities Commission, the Commission for Racial Equality or the National Disability Council and legal action may be taken. However, if you want to recruit people from minority groups, including women, you can take positive action to do this. Chapter 10 gives a brief review of the relevant law in this area.

Investigate

Does your organization provide application forms for potential jobholders? If so, do the design of the form and the headings it uses come up to standard?

Summary

The staff you recruit may well be with you for a long time. They are likely to have to cope with increasing change and flexibility in their jobs, to have to acquire new skills and take on different responsibilities. It will also continue to be difficult to get rid of employees who are not quite right, as opposed to hopelessly incompetent. It is therefore highly desirable to obtain the right people in the first place, and recruitment processes are the first step in doing this.

As a manager, you are going to have to determine future staffing levels. To do this you should consider auditing the current skills and knowledge of existing employees. This includes analysing existing jobs and determining future skill requirements. Whether you are carrying out a Human Resource Audit or filling a job vacancy, you will need to draw up a job description which includes the title of the job, its main purpose and scope, and the main tasks involved in its performance. From this you can prepare an employee specification which specifies the essential and desirable qualities required in the jobholder; these include the relevant skills, knowledge, experience and attitudes necessary to perform the job.

Recruitment of suitable candidates may take place internally or externally and can be undertaken in a number of ways. The commonest of these, especially for external candidates, is by advertising. Any advertisement needs to be designed to attract the attention, interest and desire of potential applicants, and lead them to take action to apply. It also needs to give essential information about the job, act as a filter for unsuitable candidates and conform with the legislation governing unlawful discrimination. Finally, you need to decide which format of application you will use and prepare a comprehensive set of further particulars for enquirers.

Activities

1 Job analysis. Using two or more of the methods suggested in this chapter, choose the job of someone for whom you have responsibility and conduct a job analysis.
2 Job description. Draw up a job description, based on the job analysis you have just conducted.
3 Employee specification. From the job description, draw up an employee specification under the headings suggested.
4 Recruitment advertising. Design a recruitment advertisement from the job description and employee specification which will attract the right candidates.
5 Application format. Design an application form for the job in question which will provide you with the information you need to make a decision about whether or not to short-list individuals for the selection process.

CHAPTER 4

Selection and induction

INTRODUCTION

Once you have attracted the right candidates, you move into the next phase of recruitment, which is the selection of the right person for the job. Selection can be defined as choosing the best person for the job from among candidates who come from within the organization or from outside. It involves setting up fair selection processes which, as far as possible, are designed to predict how an individual will behave at work and whether he or she can perform a specific range of tasks adequately. We now look at the advantages and disadvantages of different methods of selection and give an overview of the selection process, and follow this by taking a look at the induction process, an area which is too often under-estimated or taken for granted:

- Short-listing candidates.
- The selection process.
- Interviewing candidates.
- Other selection methods.
- Selection for other purposes.
- Non-discriminatory selection.
- Induction.

SHORT-LISTING CANDIDATES

If you are faced with an enormous pile of applications, many of which seem to have come from candidates who do not have the essential qualities for the job, then your recruitment process has failed. Think how much that has cost you and other people in terms of your time;

and how much more it is going to cost you in sorting through the applications, writing to unsuitable candidates and, perhaps, at the end of the day, having to start the whole process over again because you have failed to attract a suitable candidate. It is also bad practice because it has raised unrealistic expectations in the applicants that they might be suitable for the job you have advertised.

However, let us assume you have attracted a reasonable field of possible candidates. You now have to look at each application carefully and measure it against the 'essential' and 'desirable' qualities you identified in your employee specification.

Take the essential qualities first. Obviously, you should be interested in any candidates who fulfil all the essential requirements for the job, and less interested in those who only fulfil part of them. Selection also involves rejection. When it comes to rejecting applicants, it is both morally and practically right to let them know why they have been rejected. Look at the two extracts from letters to unsuccessful applicants below and decide which you would rather receive if you were in their place.

'We were very interested in your application for the post of . . . in this organization, but are sorry to have to tell you that you have been unsuccessful in being short-listed.'

'Thank you for your application for the post of . . . As you know from the information we sent to you, we need someone who is a fluent German speaker since this particular job involves negotiating with managers in our branches in Bonn and Berlin, many of whom do not speak English. In your application, you state that you do not speak or read German and I am afraid that this is an essential part of the job.'

The blow – and any letter of rejection is a blow to the receiver's hopes and pride – is softened in the second example since there is a clear reason given why the person cannot fulfil the requirements of this particular job. It also demonstrates that your application form needs to pin-point the essential qualities of the job or you may be turning someone down on insufficient evidence. Since your recruitment procedure was designed to attract good applicants, you may be turning someone away who might have potential for another job in your organization. If you take time to write personal letters to unsuccessful candidates, both at this stage and after you have made a final decision between short-listed candidates, you are more likely to create goodwill in all applicants who will be encouraged to apply again in the future. Some organizations now insist on the completion of a form at this stage which gives individual reasons for not short listing all applicants. If you do not give adequate reasons for not short-listing people for further selection, you run the risk of being accused – rightly or wrongly – of discrimination on grounds not related to the job in question.

Having rejected those applicants who do not fulfil your essential requirements, you may choose to offer the rest a chance to take part in the selection process or, if the numbers are too great, continue to short-list on the basis of 'desirable' qualities. But this requires some kind of objective priority-setting: are any of these qualities more desirable than others? You may need to prioritize your list of desirable qualities before making a final decision.

Once you have reduced your list of applicants to a manageable size, you may also want to call up references unless these were included with the application. If you have ever been asked to write a reference yourself, you will know how difficult it is, particularly for someone whose work is barely adequate or worse. If you fail to give a 'good' reference, that person will not get another job and you may be stuck with them. So treat references with caution; on a scale which measures the predictive validity of different selection methods, references rate just above astrology, graphology and chance.

This person joins you as he leaves us – fired with enthusiasm.

A graduate was awarded damages of £25,000 because she failed to secure employment as a result of a negligent reference from her college.

THE SELECTION PROCESS

In order to let applicants know about the selection process, what form it will take and what will be required of them, you need to have designed this at the recruitment stage. What choices are open to you?

Obviously, the method or methods of selection you choose need to be able to predict future performance in the job as much as possible. But this is not always, or even generally, the reason why people choose one method over another. Other factors such as experience and cost-effectiveness also have an effect and, despite the evidence against them, interviews are still the most commonly used method.

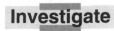 **Investigate**   What selection methods are used in your organization?

THE INTERVIEW

The selection interview has had a bad press; from 1920 onwards, psychologists and management researchers have demonstrated that interviews are both unreliable and invalid as predictors of future performance. They have proved that:

- Interviewers often make up their minds about a candidate within the first five minutes of the interview and – consciously or unconsciously – spend the rest of the interview trying to justify their judgement.
- Interviewers' judgements of candidates can be affected by their appearance, speech, gender and race either positively or negatively; people tend to favour others whom they perceive to be like themselves.
- Few interviewers have undertaken any training in interview skills.
- Research on memory shows that we remember information we hear at the beginning and end of an interview and, thus, tend to forget vital details and facts given in the middle.
- It is impossible for the human brain to concentrate at the same level over a prolonged period; thus if you are interviewing several candidates on the same day, they may not receive equal amounts of your attention.
- Finally, the British Psychological Society has found that even well-conducted interviews are only 25 per cent better than choosing someone by sticking a pin in a list of candidates!

The Board of Admirals . . . sought to establish a service connection. The ideal candidate would reply to a question such as, 'Are you any relation to Admiral Parker?' with, 'Yes, Admiral Parker is my uncle. My father is Captain Foley, my grandfather Commodore Foley. My mother's father was Admiral Hardy. Commander Hardy is my uncle. My eldest brother is a Lieutenant in the Royal Marines, my next brother is a cadet at Dartmouth and my younger brother wears a sailor suit.' 'Ah!' the senior Admiral would say. 'And what made you think of joining the Navy?' (Parkinson, 1986)

Despite all the evidence against interviews, they remain the most widely used method of selection for two reasons: first, they are relatively inexpensive, and secondly, many people feel a strong need to meet and talk to someone before appointing them. Moreover, they may still be better than the alternatives. So, if you decide that an interview is going to be part of your selection process, you will need to make it as reliable and valid a selection method as possible. There are four main factors which can affect the success or failure of a selection interview:

1   The amount of preparation before the interview.
2   The conduct and form of the interview.
3   The kinds of questions the interviewer asks.
4   The quality of the final decision-making process.

1 Preparation

A large part of the necessary preparation for the interview should already have been carried out by drawing up an employee specification and matching applications against this. However, it is unlikely that there is a perfect match against all the essential and desirable qualities in your employee specification and the interview should be designed to identify individual candidates' strengths and weaknesses. There may also be information available on how candidates have performed in other selection methods, such as those outlined later in this chapter; information on their achievements in assessment centres for example, or results of psychometric testing. All relevant information on each candidate should be collected and analysed before interviews take place (Figure 4.1).

> A Health Authority was taken to court for not interviewing a well-qualified black nursing officer. They were unable to prove that the applicant did not fulfil the requirements of the post because they had not drawn up an employee specification.

You will need to identify which areas you need to question in detail from what you already know about the candidate's relevant skills, knowledge, experience and attitudes; and the important word there is 'relevant'. It is easy in the interview itself to be side-tracked into

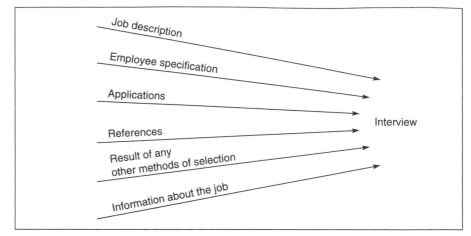

Figure 4.1
Information you
need before the
interview.

discussions of common interest or enthusiasm and to forget about
more important issues.

Your objective at the interview is to obtain as much relevant and
accurate information about the candidate as possible as objectively as
possible and you also need to second-guess what kinds of questions
candidates are likely to ask. These might include questions about
salary scales, career progression, opportunities for staff training and
development, holiday entitlement and so on. As the interviewer you
will need to be prepared, as far as possible, to give the answers.

Unless you aim to put candidates at their ease, you will not get the
best out of them. Some organizations hold what are called 'stress
interviews', designed to put candidates under pressure in order that
the interviewer can see how they react, but there are serious ethical
considerations here.

Remember that the candidate is likely to be feeling apprehensive
about the interview and try to arrange the seating so that it is as
informal as possible; avoid sitting behind a table or a desk since this
immediately creates a barrier between you and the person being
interviewed. When the candidate arrives or is shown in, start by trying
to put him or her at ease; do not launch straight into the interview
itself. Spend a few moments on general and 'safe' issues such as how
the candidate got there or the weather.

'When I got to the place, I was shown into a room with several other
people and asked to wait. It was really embarrassing. We all knew we'd
come after the same job so we didn't look at each other – imagine six or
seven people staring at spaces on the wall because they didn't want

anyone to think they were looking at them. I had to wait for fifty minutes; they must have told everyone to come at the same time.'

'When I went into the manager's office, he had this huge desk and I had to sit in front of it. It was like being back at school and I felt I'd done something wrong before I even started. He didn't smile at me, or even say "Good morning", just "Why do you want this job?" It was so unexpected, my mind just went blank. I didn't get the job but I wouldn't have wanted to work there anyway.' (Job applicant)

2 Form and conduct of the interview

Your main decision in this area is about who should be involved in the actual interviews. One-to-one interviews are less threatening to potential candidates than panel interviews but they have disadvantages in that only one person makes the decision and each interviewer has no opportunity to listen to candidates' answers if there are other interviewers involved. Large panels (of more than four or five) allow less time for individual questioning and demand more time when it comes to making selection decisions; they are also very threatening to candidates and cost more money. However, recent research on the interview as a method of selection indicates that panel interviews are the best approach in terms of the validity of decisions made but least popular with candidates. Whatever form of interview you decide to use, if it involves other people they will need to have all the essential information about the candidate beforehand and they should meet to discuss how they will handle the main areas of questioning. They should also agree on the conduct of the interview.

If there is to be a panel, it will need a Chair who will be responsible for welcoming and introducing each candidate, for ensuring that all the major points have been covered by the other members of the panel and for summarizing at the end of the interview. The Chair will also be responsible for ensuring that the final decision is made and communicated to the successful and unsuccessful candidates. In some organizations, candidates are interviewed by more than one panel.

Some selection specialists advocate complex scoring systems based on point systems like those devised by Rodger (1952) (Seven Point Plan) or Fraser (1978) (Five-fold Grading System), but any scoring system needs to relate closely to those qualities you identified in the employee specification. In many people's opinion, both Rodger's and Fraser's systems have serious defects and are open to discriminatory practices. You might like to devise a scoring system based on the specification but you should consult with, and agree the ratings with, other interviewers beforehand. It can be an aid to objectivity if properly designed, agreed and adhered to.

Investigate

What kind, or kinds of selection interviewing does your organization practise?

3 Questions asked by the interviewer

Your preparation and discussion with other people involved in the interview process should have identified the areas you need to question for each candidate. It is not enough merely to have a general set of questions which are asked of all candidates, although these may be a starting-point. You should treat each candidate as a separate individual, with different characteristics from the others. Thus if a candidate is clearly under-qualified or indeed over-qualified (and this latter is not as uncommon as might be thought) you will need to raise these during the questioning.

In the interview itself there are ways of asking questions that will elicit the answers you require and there are also questions you should not ask. Not unnaturally, many candidates are nervous when they come for an interview and have some difficulty in putting themselves across. You can help them in the way you phrase your questions. You can make a choice, depending on what kind of answer you are looking for, between any of the following:

- **Open questions** – which are designed to draw the candidate out such as, 'Will you tell me about how you set up a networking system in your last job?' or 'Can you tell me more about this training course you went on last year?' or 'What appeals to you about this job?'
- **Closed questions** – used to clarify a point of fact and which often only require a short or single word answer. For example, 'Did you head up the team?' or 'Was that your own idea?' or 'Did you or your employer decide to do that?'
- **Hypothetical questions** – which can be used to find out how a candidate might respond in certain situations such as 'If we offered you this job, how would you go about improving communications between departments?' or 'If you had a budget of £100,000 for promoting a new product, how would you spend it?'

■ **Probing questions** – which are necessary if you feel a candidate has not given you a full answer and you want to find out more. They can be used immediately after a candidate has referred to something you would like to know more about by saying 'Exactly what happened next …?' or you can return to an earlier point by saying, for example, 'I'd like to go back to something you said earlier about not enjoying your work on the project team. Could you tell me why you didn't enjoy it?'
■ **Reflective questions** – which are designed to encourage the candidate to reflect on an experience and consider how he or she might have dealt with the situation in a different way.

A poor questioning technique is when an interviewer asks a multiple question such as:

'Tell me how you got your present job, what attracted you to it and which parts of it you like best and which parts you like least. Do you prefer it to the job you had before that?'

This leaves the candidate confused as to which part of the question should be answered first and both the candidate and the interviewer are likely to forget all the parts of the original question.

Questions you should not ask include those of a personal nature which are not relevant to the job and/or could be described as **discriminatory**. For example:

■ 'How old are you?'
■ 'Are you married? What does your partner do?'
■ 'What religious holidays do you observe?'
■ What arrangements do you have for child care?'

The following question was asked of an African woman with impeccable qualifications, applying for the job of personnel officer in a well-known company.

'Mrs X, we have a problem. People around here are not used to working with black people. If we gave you this job, how would you cope?'

The Commission for Racial Equality and the Equal Opportunities Commission both have information about basic principles of non-discriminatory questioning in selection interviews.

Do not ask questions which are likely to take the candidate a long time to answer such as 'Tell me about your previous jobs . . .'. Avoid questions which are designed to give you the answer you want rather than the real answer, such as 'Wouldn't it have been more efficient if you had brought in a specialist to deal with that part of the job?' or 'You don't like working on your own, do you?'

Ideally, the candidate should do most of the talking so avoid getting into interesting discussions of your pet subject or reminiscences of your own experiences. Do not probe on sensitive or emotional issues unless these are truly relevant to the job.

Finally, it is ethically wrong to raise expectations of success in a candidate's mind by asking questions which imply that he or she will get the job: always preface questions about how they would act in the job with a phrase such as 'If you got this job . . .'.

An interviewing technique which uses examples from the candidate's own past experience to focus on the skills needed for another job is called **behavioural interviewing**. For example, if you had analysed a job which you felt required quick decision-making, the ability to work under pressure and the need for diplomatic handling of problems, you might ask questions like the following:

- 'Give me an example of a time when you had to make a decision quickly.'
- 'Can you describe any job you have held where you were faced with problems and pressures which tested your ability to cope?'
- 'Can you give me an example of a time when you had to conform to a policy with which you did not agree?'

Some candidates, often through nervousness, will talk endlessly and pointlessly if given the chance. You will need to bring them back to the point courteously, perhaps rephrase the question or move on to another area. It is perfectly acceptable for you and other interviewers to take notes during the interview; in fact it is preferable if you are interviewing more than one person on the same day. It is a good idea to explain to the candidates that you intend to do this as an aid to decision-making, but try not to make your note-taking obvious, particularly when probing sensitive areas.

When you have asked all the questions you feel are necessary, you should give each candidate an opportunity to ask questions of you and other interviewers. Do not be surprised if they cannot think of any; again, nervousness and the effort of concentrating on your questions may have caused them to forget what they wanted to ask. You might even make some suggestions such as 'Is there anything you would like to ask us about the job itself, or the organization? Anything about wages or holidays or shift hours or ...?' Of course, most of this information should have been covered in your Information Pack but candidates may have concerns which they need to raise at this point.

You should be careful not to make promises to candidates which cannot be fulfilled, such as assurances about training and promotion if they take the job. Apart from being morally wrong to promise something which, later, cannot be provided, employees will be resentful if they feel they took the job under false pretences. Sometimes, interviewers are so keen to appoint a particularly outstanding candidate that they make offers, often in good faith, to encourage the person to join the organization; later, when the offers do not materialize, the dissatisfied employee may feel bitter enough to make a formal complaint.

Finally, when closing the interview, thank the candidates for coming and let them know when and how they can expect to learn the outcome.

4 Making a decision

Despite all your efforts at obtaining the best range of candidates, briefing other interviewers and controlling the interview itself, it is likely that when it comes to making a choice out of say, six candidates, that different interviewers will have made different choices. If your recruitment and short-listing processes have been effective, this is inevitable since the choice will have been narrowed down to a few very good candidates. The decision-making process needs to be managed in the same way as the other elements of recruitment and selection since the eventual judgement is the culmination of all that has gone before. It has to be rational, explicable and unbiased and based as far as possible on objective criteria.

One way of looking at this process is by analysing why you would NOT appoint certain candidates – this is useful since you should explain to unsuccessful candidates the reasons why they were not selected and, again, your organization may require these reasons to be given in writing for their own records. Here, your employee specification and analysis of essential and desirable qualities for performance of the job should be used as your benchmarks.

Once a decision has been reached, the successful candidate should be offered the job and those who were unsuccessful need to be told. Again, bear in mind that these unsuccessful candidates might be successful in future and give as much feedback as possible as to why each failed to get the job. Remember, too, that a verbal acceptance of a job is not legally binding and, until the candidate has formally accepted a job offer in writing, he or she might change their mind.

Investigate

Think back to a selection interview in which you were involved. How far did it reflect the 'good practice' suggested here?

OTHER SELECTION METHODS

Alternative or complementary methods of selection include a range of psychometric tests, the use of biodata and the use of assessment centres. In addition, there are a number of less well known and less reliable methods involving the analysis of handwriting, astrology and honesty testing (or lie detecting). Self-assessment and peer assessment have also been used but are also considered to be unreliable.

Research has shown that psychometric tests, which include work sampling, tests of ability and personality tests, can be more reliable than interviewing providing the test is relevant to the job which has to be performed and that the tester has been trained in its use. Biodata, which is short for 'biographical data' is a relatively recent selection technique which appears to have high predictive validity and can be cost-effective; however, it is more suitable for organizations that have a large number of vacancies for the same type of job and it does require specialist training in its administration. Assessment centres are not places but processes, involving candidates being assessed on various job-related tests by a range of assessors. They are considered to be valid, reliable and fair as a means of selecting people and, again, require trained assessors.

Psychometric testing

There is a vast range of tests available on the open market and one must be cautious in assessing their predictive value. Some large organizations that rely heavily on testing in their selection and promotion procedures are finding that different departments are using different tests and that decisions are being made independently of any corporate strategy. Similarly, only chartered occupational psychologists are qualified to train people in applying and analysing most worthwhile tests and there is a growth in amateur consultancy and 'easy to use, no training required' short personality tests in this area; these are usually unreliable. Nevertheless, the use of psychometric testing, usually used in conjunction with interviews rather than by itself, has increased in recent years.

Undergraduates and others who attend a number of job selections which involve aptitude and personality tests, have often carried out the same test several times before. Experience shows that individuals' performance on aptitude tests improves significantly when they undergo the same, or similar, tests more than once.

A Coventry health trust discontinued the use of computerized personality testing in job selection after five black nurses claimed the tests discriminated against them. They were awarded a total of £35,000 in an out-of-court settlement.

Psychological tests

These include ability tests, covering both physical and mental ability, personality tests and tests of motivation. In some cases, they may also include tests of a medical or fitness nature if there are particular physical requirements of the job. Ability tests usually focus on mental abilities such as verbal, numerical and spatial abilities and specific tests have been developed for computer programmers, systems analysts, people working on word processors and those who work in automated offices.

The Civil Aviation Authority, which recruits over 200 people a year as air traffic controllers, uses computer-based simulation as part of their recruitment and selection process.

Recent developments in ability testing have increased their sensitivity to individual levels of ability and the more sophisticated ones can be used to differentiate between adequate and higher level candidates. Again, use of these tests has grown in recent years.

Personality tests relate to, for example, the degree to which a person can be categorized as extrovert or introvert, as stable or neurotic, as dependent or independent. It is the author's opinion that there needs to be a clear rationale for asking candidates to undertake a personality test as part of the selection process unless (a) the outcome of the test(s) is essential to predicting adequate performance in the job, (b) the test is proved to be non-discriminatory in terms of gender, race, creed or disability and (c) the person who is administering and analysing the results has been professionally trained.

Work sampling is a test which attempts to replicate some of the key elements of a job. Such tests are expensive to design unless they are going to be widely used since each work-sample has to be related to a specific job. Examples of work-sample tests for managers include:

- in-tray prioritizing exercises;
- group problem-solving exercises;
- consensus decision-making;
- role play simulations.

Biodata

Biodata methods of selection are relatively new and are based on the assumption that details of people's lives and experiences will reveal their personality and aptitudes. Candidates have to answer a very detailed questionnaire which is then scored and selection decisions are based on the scoring. They are used effectively for filtering very large numbers of applicants applying for a single job or for entry-level jobs such as management trainees. In the case of small numbers of applicants or a wide range of jobs, however, biodata can be an extremely expensive exercise.

Assessment centres

Assessment centre exercises are derived from detailed job analysis and are similar to those noted above for psychological tests. Candidates are evaluated by a number of assessors on their performance in these exercises. The resulting data are then evaluated and scores are derived for each candidate. These methods are now being widely used for appraisal and promotion within organizations as well as for selection purposes, which increases their cost-effectiveness to the organization.

These alternative methods of selection are useful in initially screening large numbers of candidates prior to a second stage, which may include interviews. They can provide additional information about candidates prior to final selection but, with the exception of assessment centres, they are rarely predictive enough in themselves. They should never be used unless they relate directly to the job role concerned and, in most cases, they require a trained professional to analyse the results.

Investigate   Does your organization use any of these alternative methods of selection? Are they administered by trained staff?

SELECTION FOR OTHER PURPOSES

Much of what has been written in this chapter also applies to selection for promotion. Although a job description and employee specification may already exist, these may be out of date and a fresh look at the job might be desirable. Internal vacancies should be advertised internally if they are open to all and, of course, there should be no hint of discrimination. The paperwork may include reports from performance reviews, appraisals or line managers/supervisors.

The form and conduct of the selection process, and the legal requirements surrounding it, should be as rigorous as that for any job vacancy in the organization. In particular, there need to be arrangements whereby unsuccessful candidates are given full feedback on their performance and, if necessary, counselling about their future career prospects.

Selection for redundancy can be a legal minefield, and the main framework of an employer's obligations is provided in Chapter 10.

INDUCTION

The first few weeks, or even days, of a worker's experience of a job can have a lasting impact on their longer-term view of it. People are at their most vulnerable at this point before they really appreciate the requirements of the job or get to know their colleagues, and it is therefore vital that they are given appropriate support through a proper induction programme. Apart from the cost of possibly having to replace someone who rapidly decides that they have no future in an organization that ignores them when they arrive, it is also difficult for their colleagues who have to deal with somebody who is disoriented.

Induction might be said to consist of three rather separate sets of activities: an introduction to the organization and the role; socialization or the process of adjusting to the organization; and any more formal training and development necessary for the job. The introduction to the organization may well be partly at the organizational level, with various contractual, payments, pension and similar dimensions of becoming an employee; with this there may also be something like an organization video to explain the wider organization to incomers, and probably various explanatory documents. But there will also be an introduction to immediate colleagues and people in other sub-units with whom there may be a work relationship. And most of all there will be a welcoming meeting with the immediate manager to clarify responsibilities and to reconcile expectations on both sides.

One company which makes its induction programme explicit, expects the following list of tasks to have been completed during an employee's first week:

- Introduction to team
- Outline of area and team's functions and activities
- Office layout
- Explanation of working hours
- Holiday arrangements and entitlement
- Standard of dress
- Fire drill procedures
- Absence procedures
- Smoking rules
- Accidents at work and first aid
- Use of telephone regarding personal calls
- Security and ID
- Business confidentiality and integrity
- Discrimination
- Outline of grievance procedures
- Outline of disciplinary procedures
- Who our customers are

- Responsibility towards customers
- Explanation of the training programme

Each item is 'signed off' by the employee's line manager.

This introduction is followed by an equally important next stage of socialization, in which the incomer begins to understand his or her colleagues as individuals and personalities rather than just names, and begins to understand the informal norms, values and processes of the unit and the organization. This latter is often forgotten in the induction programme, and is best taken into account by appointing a mentor or at least a 'buddy' to whom the new employee can turn for advice and who can take a pro-active approach to assisting in the socialization process. But while the newcomer can be helped to adjust, there is much that can only be done by themselves. It might be suggested that there are four steps in socialization:

- Confronting and accepting reality
- Achieving role clarity
- Coming to terms with the context
- Detecting signposts of successful socialization

The third stage is the initial training and development any employee deserves on joining the organization. It will in large part be about the demands of the specific job, but should also relate the job to other aspects of the organization.

As part of its effort to improve customer service, Wessex Water Authority introduced a six-week induction programme for all its customer service staff. The programme included field training, with staff working with plumbers and sewer repair teams to find out what the jobs entailed. There were sessions on the company's water, sewerage and billing systems as well as training on dealing with customers. The staff welcomed the programme and felt more confident about dealing with a much wider range of enquiries than they had before.

Induction is rarely given to temporary or short-term staff in the misguided belief that they will not care much about the organization as a whole and that they are just there to do the job. However, many organizations rely heavily on part-time or temporary staff and use them on a regular basis. These staff also need training if they are going to be effective.

TNT Express Worldwide has a policy of encouraging long-term relationships with temporary clerical support staff so that they will come back when the company needs them. Where possible, TNT provides practical 'hands-on' experience of the job for which temporary help is needed and new staff are introduced to the place and the people where they will be working. They are given a copy of the company's manual, 'Welcome to TNT' and a copy of the company's quality strategy.

Investigate

What induction do you and your organization provide for new staff? Is it adequate? How might it be improved?

Summary

Selection is not an easy process to get right, and there are strong disadvantages to all the available methods. Nevertheless, interviews are still the most prevalent method of selection, although increasingly supplemented by psychometric and psychological tests.

Induction is a frequently underestimated part of the process of getting new employees established in their jobs, but nevertheless one which is vitally necessary if they are to be effective and motivated workers.

Activities

1 Imagine that you have been asked to take part in or lead a selection interview for a post in your area of responsibility. Choose a particular post and note down the essential questions you would ask candidates.
2 Write a short letter to an unsuccessful candidate who was short-listed for a post but failed to be appointed. How would you word such a letter so that the candidate felt that he or she had been given a fair assessment?
3 Develop an induction plan for a worker newly joining your area of responsibility.

CHAPTER 5

Motivation, job satisfaction and job design

▌ INTRODUCTION

On any day as a manager, you are likely to have to 'manage' other people on a one-to-one basis. This involves understanding people as individuals and recognizing their differences as well as drawing up some general principles for managing them.

As managers, we need to understand why people choose to perform satisfactorily or unsatisfactorily; why some people appear to be committed to their jobs and others are often absent or unwell. We need to find out what rewards and incentives individuals value so that, where possible, we can provide these. In short, we need to provide motivation for the people for whom we are responsible.

The job itself and the way in which it is designed can act as a significant motivating (or de-motivating) force in individuals. Every job has specific demands and the person who carries out that job will need certain skills and abilities to achieve the expected level of performance. This is why we suggested in Chapter 3 that you carried out a Human Resource Audit – perhaps the wrong people are in the wrong jobs. If they are, then they are not likely to be experiencing job satisfaction.

In this chapter we will be considering:

■ Individual behaviour at work.
■ Motivation.

- Job satisfaction.
- Job design.
- Characteristics of a well-designed job.
- Designing or redesigning the jobs of your staff.
- Alternative methods of organizing work.

INDIVIDUAL BEHAVIOUR AT WORK

What do you think about the other people you work with - your boss, your subordinates and your colleagues? How do you know that the way you think about other people is shared by them? And what is their opinion about you? To manage people effectively, you need to clear your mind of your own beliefs, opinions and assumptions since they are highly personal to you. You and your boss may have quite different ideas about how *A* performs his or her job or how reliable *B* is, and these may be different again from the ideas of some of your colleagues. Nobody is necessarily 'right' or 'wrong' in their opinions, providing these are based on facts rather than on personal beliefs. Think of some of the idiosyncratic ways people think about others.

'I never trust anyone who wears brightly coloured ties.'

'She's got two young children so she'll always be asking for time off.'

'He's joined the same golf club as Simon – must be looking for promotion.'

'You should see her desk – it's a tip. I'd never ask her to take on organizing anything serious.'

You could say some of these statements were based on 'facts', but they are hardly objective, nor do the opinions stated necessarily follow from the observations.

Investigate

Think back to any recent discussions you have had with other people at work. Did any of them make statements like those above? Did you?

Wrightsman, in his book *Assumptions about Human Nature* (1974), identified six categories of belief on which people based their assumptions about others. These are given below and you might like to try to place your own beliefs about other people in relation to each category.

Wrightsman stated that everyone had certain general beliefs about other people and the degree to which they were trustworthy, unselfish, nonconformist (or independent) and rational. They also believed other people shared their values (or not) and that, in general, others were fairly simple, or fairly complex, human beings (Figure 5.1).

	1	2	3	4	5	
Trustworthy						Untrustworthy
Unselfish						Selfish
Noncomformist						Conformist
Rational						Irrational
Same values						Different values
Simple						Complex

Figure 5.1
Wrightsman's
five-point scale of
beliefs

Investigate

If you identified your own set of beliefs using Wrightsman's categories, you might like to try them out on someone else and see how closely you match each other's ways of thinking about other people.

Another reason why people behave differently in a work situation is, quite simply, because they have different abilities and experience. In Chapter 4 you considered assessment centres as a form of selection; assessment centres and other tests measure ability which differentiates one individual from another. Some people will always rate 'better' than others in terms of mental or physical ability. They may not choose to use that ability at work, perhaps because they find the job unsatisfying, boring or beneath their ability, or because it does not allow them to use a particular area of ability. My son once scored extremely highly on a test of spatial ability, yet has never had a job in which he could use this particular talent.

However, the identification of a particular level of ability does not mean that you can predict how that person will behave at work although it has been proved that most top managers are of above average intelligence – but not in the genius class (Hunt, 1979). It is just another piece of the jigsaw that makes up an individual. Another, more complex piece, is the kind of experience the individual has had. If you think about it, we have all had individual experiences of life before and outside work. Some of these may appear to be similar, such as the type of school attended, or the kind of houses people live in, but most of each individual's experience will be specific to that person. Everyone brings with them a whole clutch of different experiences which affect how they behave and perform at work.

Experience at work also affects how people behave. Take the example of a meeting between, say, the production manager, the sales manager and the company accountant. A discussion might go as follows:

Sales manager: 'I'm getting a lot of complaints from customers about our long delivery times – we're going to lose out to the competition. Mitchells can guarantee delivery in 10 days; we're lucky if the customer gets stuff from us under three weeks. You've got to increase production or we'll all be looking for new jobs.

Production manager: That's all very well. I can't increase production until we get two new machines and the people to operate them – it's as simple as that. Give me the machines and the staff – you'll get your shorter delivery.

Accountant: 'We can't afford new machines at the moment – you know that. Not until sales pick up, and the current figures aren't promising. You'll need to get your sales staff working harder ...'

Deadlock. Each person has a perfectly valid argument, yet they are each approaching the problem from the different viewpoints of their work experience. People can also find difficulty when they change from one organization to another where the 'cultures' of those organizations are different. Someone who has worked, for example, in the Civil Service, which is highly structured and where there are rules and procedures to be followed for nearly every activity, would find it difficult to adjust to working in a voluntary organization where there is great stress on consultation and participation, even if the requirements of the job were broadly similar; their work experience would be quite different.

We all make assumptions about other people based on our own experience – it is a way of making sense of relating to others. We each set ourselves certain standards and expect other people to adhere to them, even though they may not share our views and have different standards for themselves.

MOTIVATION

Motivation has become one of the buzz-words of modern management. 'He lacks motivation', 'Jo really motivates her team – they'll do anything for her', 'We need to motivate the workforce ...'. Yet, like all human states, motivation is both highly individual and complex and there is a difference between what motivates people to perform above average and what leads to below-average performance.

Assumptions about the way people behave at work

Based on his observations of management during his years as a senior administrator in an American college, Professor Douglas McGregor suggested that managers make either Theory X or Theory Y assumptions about the way others behave. (The terms Theory X or Y are merely names McGregor (1960) used to describe the kinds of assumptions.) Theory X assumptions include the following:

- that the average human being inherently dislikes work and will avoid it if possible;
- that, because of this, subordinates must be coerced, controlled, directed or threatened with punishment to get them to put in adequate effort at work;
- that the average person prefers to be directed, wishes to avoid responsibility, has relatively little ambition and wants security above all else.

Perhaps you know of managers who have all or some of these assumptions about the people who work for them; perhaps you yourself think about some other people in this way. Theory X has had its followers for a long time and can certainly be used for explaining some kinds of behaviour in organizations. More recent research on people at work, however, supports McGregor's set of Theory Y assumptions which include the following:

- that most people do not inherently dislike work and that, according to the conditions, it may be a source of either satisfaction or punishment;
- that people will generally exercise self-direction and self-control in pursuit of objectives to which they are committed;
- that most people learn, under proper conditions, not only to accept but to seek responsibility;
- that most people are not being used by organizations to their full potential;
- that, in order to obtain commitment from employees, rewards should fulfil an individual's self-actualization needs (we will be looking at self-actualization later in this chapter).

A good relationship between employee and line manager is the most important factor for motivating staff and establishing a positive psychological contract, according to a Chartered Institute of Personnel and Development survey.

If managers choose either the set of assumptions associated with Theory X or with Theory Y, there will be a tendency throughout the organization for people to respond to the way they are managed. Therefore, if employees feel that they are not being trusted, they may behave in a less trustworthy way.

Investigate

Can you think of any examples of employees behaving in Theory X or Theory Y ways and relate this behaviour to their manager's or supervisor's assumptions about them?

The Theory Y explanation of the way we may think about other people at work included a belief about the kinds of rewards which people value. Frederick Taylor, an engineer and the exponent of the idea of 'scientific management', stated 'What the workforce want from their employers beyond anything else is high wages and what employers want from their workforce most of all is low labour costs of manufacture ... the existence or absence of these two elements forms the best index to either good or bad management' (Taylor, 1947). We all know that this assumption is outdated; although wages and the level of pay for the job are an important factor in reward systems, we can all think of people who are underpaid and yet enjoy their work and perform it effectively.

Not everyone works harder in the hope of a pay rise or a bonus. Companies like British Nuclear Fuels have bowed to pressure to reduce the working week for manual workers from 39 hours to 35. Other organizations, particularly those in the food, drink and tobacco industries, now find it necessary to offer other benefits such as increased holiday entitlement which are not directly financial.

Motivation based on satisfying individual needs

An alternative explanation of human behaviour is put forward by the psychologist Maslow, who believed there were five levels of need which the individual sought to satisfy. The lowest of these included the basic physiological needs for food, drink and shelter; once these were satisfied, individuals needed to protect themselves against danger, threat and deprivation – safety needs. Thereafter, the levels of need rose through social needs, the need for self esteem and status (ego needs) to the need for self-actualization (Figure 5.2). Maslow explained self-actualization as follows:

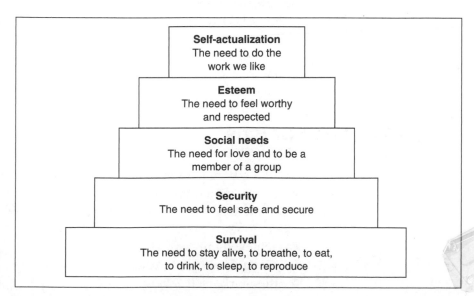

Figure 5.2
Maslow's
hierarchy of needs

> A musician must make music, an artist must paint, a poet must write, if he is to be ultimately happy. What a man can be, he must be. This need we may call self-actualization . . . It refers to the desire for self-fulfilment, namely the tendency for him to become actualized in what he is potentially . . . the desire to become more and more what one is, to become everything that one is capable of becoming. (Maslow, 1943)

Later researchers have questioned the hierarchical nature of Maslow's explanation but share in his belief that people work for different reasons and that these reasons may include financial rewards but only as part of an overall reward system.

> Surrey County Council has launched a pilot scheme that will allow 400 staff to choose from a range of benefits rather than to receive a fixed package. The benefits up for negotiation include annual leave, dental care, childcare, health screening, life assurance and salary. Employees can develop a package suited to their own needs provided the total cost remains the same. Someone might, for example, opt to take less holiday in return for a dental package.

> 'When I look at the individuals in my team, I realize how diverse they are in relation to what motivates them. They include a 25-year-old graduate trainee who is desperately keen to embark on a management career and whose sights are set very high – for him, promotion prospects and status are everything; a grandmother who is keen to earn as much as possible so that she can retire in relative comfort; a mother of young children, keen to work full time but who needs flexible hours to fit in with childcare; a man who is currently undertaking five days' work in four in order to spend the fifth day at classes because he is taking a course connected with the voluntary work he does.'

JOB SATISFACTION

Frederick Herzberg's research into the motivation of accountants and engineers revealed a number of factors which affected the way in which people felt about their work (Herzberg et al., 1959). These included:

- achievement
- recognition from others
- the work itself

- responsibility
- opportunities for advancement
- company policy and administration
- supervision
- salary
- interpersonal relations
- working conditions

Those factors which made people feel satisfied with their job and motivated them to work included high levels of achievement, recognition, opportunities for advancement and responsibility. The content of the work itself was also very important. Factors which affected employees adversely and which led them to feel dissatisfied with the work they were doing, included company policy and administration, supervision, salary, interpersonal relations and working conditions; if all or any of these were considered by individuals to be of a low standard, employees felt dissatisfied with what they were doing. Common symptoms of dissatisfaction at work include persistent lateness or absenteeism, below-average performance and real or imagined illness.

The important lesson here is that if the factors classified by Herzberg as 'dissatisfiers' can be improved and the level of the 'satisfying' or motivating factors increased, performance should improve; merely improving the 'dissatisfiers' will not result in any long-term increase in an individual's motivation to work although it may produce short-term results and will increase job satisfaction.

In a survey, the *Guardian* newspaper asked its readers which factors were important in providing job satisfaction. Amongst those considered most important were:

personal freedom;
increased responsibility;
praise from superiors;
respect from others at work.

'Making money' appeared as twenty-eighth in order of importance.

Investigate

Why do you choose to work in your present job? List your reasons in order of importance. Then ask some of your colleagues and subordinates what their reasons are – they may well be different from yours.

Having identified some general factors which can increase or decrease job satisfaction, it has to be recognized that each individual is likely to value these factors according to their own needs. For example, people with young children are likely to value the provision of childcare at work and flexible working hours more highly than people who do not have these responsibilities.

Hoechst and Roussel, the pharmaceutical companies, both had very paternalistic benefit policies – employees simply received what the company thought was best for them. When the companies merged, a taskforce was set up to look at existing and future benefit policies.

The taskforce discovered that most existing benefits, with the exception of company cars, were taken up by older employees or those with health problems. Less than 5 per cent of employees actually took advantage of pensions, medical insurance or healthcare in any one year – yet these cost the company £4.5m per annum.

Also, the work environment was changing. If there was no such thing as a 'job for life' any more, what was the point in offering benefits which depended on deferred gratification? The composition of the workforce was changing as well; there were more women, more professional part-timers, more job-sharers and more returning mothers.

Based on these findings and staff attitude surveys, Hoechst Roussel decided it needed a flexible benefits system where choice was actually a benefit in itself. Such a system would include cash-based benefits and pension schemes as well as fitness training, childcare, company cars and free parking.

Some companies have concentrated on improving job satisfaction for employees with young children. But there are others whose dependants may be elderly or infirm, people whose partners may be ill, unemployed or in prison. There is a significant minority of people with no partners and who may or may not have dependants – all of these are unlikely to benefit from childcare schemes. To a person who has a strong need for status, for example, an expensive company car is likely to bring satisfaction while another might value more free time to spend in leisure pursuits. In some cases, training incentives or a flexible retirement decade will increase job satisfaction and commitment to the organization.

As incentives to its sales-staff, Prudential Assurance offer all-expenses paid travel breaks and an annual dinner for its most successful salespeople.

Expectancy Theory

Herzberg's theory sees motivation leading to increased – or decreased – levels of job satisfaction. Job satisfaction in itself, however, will not necessarily affect performance. For performance to improve, individuals have to believe that the extra effort they put in will increase the probability of obtaining the reward they value.

In Figure 5.3, it is not the contents of the boxes which are important; it is the links which are stressed in Expectancy Theory; and, although we have used the word 'Reward' in the right-hand box, this could just as well be 'Punishment' if an individual is working harder to avoid an outcome such as disciplinary action or dismissal. According to Expectancy Theory, if we want to improve motivation at work, we need to consider:

- the link between effort and performance;
- the link between performance and reward;
- the types of rewards available.

Figure 5.3
Expectancy theory: the links between effort, performance and reward

Figure 5.4 describes some of the factors which can affect the link between effort and performance. It is all very well for someone to expend extra effort, but they also need to have the abilities to perform the job, as well as resources such as time, equipment and money. They need to know what they have to achieve (objectives) and they need some kind of recognition that their performance has improved. If any of these are missing, then performance is likely to be adversely affected.

Figure 5.4
Factors affecting the link between effort and performance

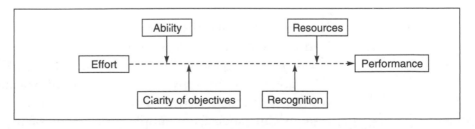

We have already discussed the link between performance and reward and the need for the reward to be meaningful and valued by the individual. Rewards don't always need to be tangible, such as bonus payments, promotion or other benefits. These are *extrinsic* rewards because they depend on someone else. Intrinsic rewards, however, are those feelings which result directly from performance of a task − rewards such as a sense of achievement, of having done a good job, of having done the job better than it was done before, of having done something worthwhile. Of course, intrinsic outcomes are not always rewarding; you can experience feelings of fatigue, frustration or disappointment as a result of performing a job less well than you had hoped.

If the job has been well done and the rewards are both appropriate and fair, this will lead to job satisfaction. And, if you look at Figure 5.5, it is this effect on job satisfaction which is most likely to lead to sustained or improved effort.

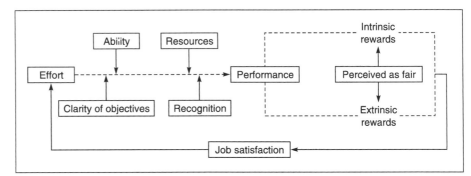

Figure 5.5
The relationship between the factors affecting motivation

Investigate

What kinds of motivational rewards does your organization offer and how much influence can you have on providing valued rewards for above-average performance?

Pay as a motivator

Herzberg identified the level of pay as one of the factors which could lead to dissatisfaction at work rather than one which contributed in any major way to job satisfaction and motivation. Yet, financial incentives are often the only reward organizations and their managers provide to induce increased performance. Performance-related pay systems can range from simple bonuses or salary/wage increases to more sophisticated pay systems such as time rates, payment by results (PBR), measured day work or profit sharing. Whatever the system, it is vital that it suits the circumstances of the organization and its ability to operate it successfully, and that it is participated in willingly by employees and their trade unions. It needs continual monitoring and evaluation to ensure it is fulfilling its purpose.

To be successful, performance-related pay schemes need to be based on performance management which links objectives, behaviours, competences and skills to organizational requirements. It needs to be fully understood by all employees who are affected by the scheme and, if possible, introduced with their agreement. On its own, a performance-related pay scheme can be unsuccessful; it should form part of an overall reward philosophy which meets individual and organizational needs. We will be discussing other aspects of rewards in Chapter 8.

Maxfax introduced an incentive scheme based on team financial rewards. Alli's team were excited at the prospect and decided to use the money – if they achieved their targets – to go as a group on a weekend trip to EuroDisney. They all put in extra effort and, as a result, achieved the targets necessary to get the bonus. There was a tremendous sense of achievement and heightened team spirit as they discussed the details of their proposed trip. Meanwhile, Alli had just learned from their line manager that the money wasn't available because it hadn't been accounted for in the relevant budget year . . .

JOB DESIGN

Much of the early work on designing jobs was undertaken in the 1970s by companies such as Saab, United Biscuits and ICI who were pioneers in experimenting with job redesign and work reorganization. Although these organizations aimed at improving job satisfaction, their 'hidden agenda' was to improve productivity. However, as you have seen, increased job satisfaction will not always result in increased performance. There are other, related factors such as appropriate reward systems to be considered.

By increasing job satisfaction, however, there are a number of advantages to the organization, to the manager and to the individual employee as set out in the Figure 5.6.

Organizational benefits

When employees are satisfied with the work they are doing and with the work environment, they identify more closely with the employing

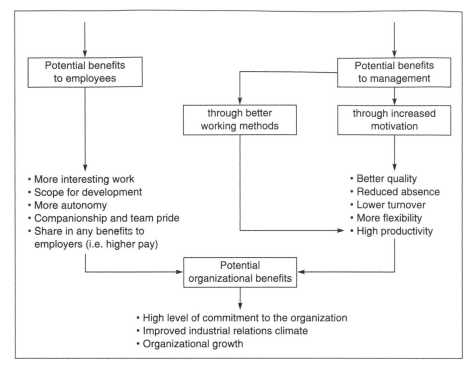

Figure 5.6
Improving job design and work organization to meet individual needs (*The Effective Manager*, Book 4, Open University, 1996)

organization. Organizations cannot buy loyalty yet they constantly wish to foster it. Employees who are committed to the organization are likely to work harder towards organizational goals, seize opportunities and new ideas and act as good public relations officers for their employers. There is less chance of industrial unrest since employees have little dissatisfaction and the organization as a whole can expect to survive and grow.

Management benefits

With highly motivated staff, managers can expect better quality performance than from subordinates who are dissatisfied with the work they are doing. The symptoms of dissatisfaction, such as absenteeism and illness, will not be present and they are likely to discover that staff are more willing and able to perform a range of jobs if their individual skills and abilities are fully developed. In turn, this should lead to improved productivity and better quality service.

Individual benefits

If a person with particular skills and abilities finds his or her job suited to those qualities, the work they are doing will be more interesting and, thus, less likely to produce stress. Repetitive and boring work is, in fact, highly stressful, particularly if it involves little opportunity for moving about. The job should have some scope for development of the individual so that he or she can see opportunities for improvement and advancement. With more control over the work, the individual has an increased sense of autonomy and freedom as to the way in which it can be carried out.

However, these are *potential* benefits and you should not expect, just by re-designing a job, that all of them will naturally occur. There are, as usual, a number of other factors to be considered such as the expectations and abilities of individuals, the kind of organization in which you work and its reward systems and, finally, the kind of work which has to be performed. Although we will be looking at alternative ways of performing jobs later in this chapter, most of us work under certain constraints, not least the expectations and demands of our bosses, customers or clients.

CHARACTERISTICS OF A WELL-DESIGNED JOB

The main work on job design was carried out in the 1970s by Hackman and Oldham (1976), who developed a set of five core job dimensions or job characteristics; these were the essential ingredients of a well-designed job and, in an ideal situation, all five should be present. If they were, Hackman and Oldham argued, the individual would feel the job was meaningful, would have a sense of personal responsibility for the outcomes of the job and would, through feedback on performance, be personally strengthened and motivated to improve. The overall result would be high-quality work performance, high internal work motivation and satisfaction for the individual and reduced absenteeism and staff turnover.

Hackman and Oldham's core job characteristics consisted of:

- Skill variety
- Task identity
- Task significance
- Autonomy
- Feedback

Skill variety

This characteristic refers to the extent to which a job requires a variety of activities so that the individual can use a number of different skills and talents. Not everyone enjoys jobs with a high degree of variety, however; some people prefer a more routinized job with which they feel 'safe' and able to cope. Others prefer as wide a variety as possible, providing they have the skills to undertake these or can be provided with necessary training and development.

Task identity

Some jobs are less satisfying than others because, not only do they use few of the jobholder's skills and abilities, but the job itself forms only a small part of a whole. The person doing the job cannot see its outcome in concrete terms. Assembly-line work, where an operator is only responsible for a small task such as welding together two pieces of metal or screwing several nuts on to passing bolts, has little task identity unless the person can see their part in the final outcome. Experiments with changing from an assembly line production method to one where each person puts together a whole or a major part of the finished product have been very successful in increasing job satisfaction – and output. Individuals become responsible for overall quality as well as the manual tasks involved.

Task significance

How important is your job to the organization? Or mine? Or the job of one of your subordinates? How 'good' do they feel about the jobs they are doing? Task significance relates to the extent to which the job has a substantial impact on the lives and work of other people either within the work environment or outside it. People who work for voluntary organizations such as Oxfam, for example, and are unwaged, are usually highly motivated because they feel that the work they are doing has a significant impact on others who are less fortunate than themselves. Hackman and Oldham cite the example of people who tighten nuts on aircraft brake assemblies; they are likely to see their work as more meaningful in terms of the overall safety of the aeroplane, its crew and passengers than someone who fills small boxes with paper clips even though the skill levels are similar.

The significance of the job will, again, depend on the individual's personal values which is why some people choose to work for Oxfam, or teach children with learning difficulties or take up nursing while others elect to program computers, drive long-distance lorries or sell designer clothes. In each case, it is the extent to which the person is satisfied by the task that he or she is doing that is important.

Investigate

To what extent does your own job have skill variety, task identity and task significance?

It is possible, according to Hackman and Oldham, for one of the above factors to be missing and for the job still to be satisfying.

Autonomy

Autonomy refers to the amount of freedom and discretion the individual can exercise over the job. A job with high autonomy is likely to engender a sense of responsibility – which Herzberg (1968) identified as being one of the main elements affecting job satisfaction – providing that person wants and can cope with this. Some people prefer jobs with a low level of responsibility where they are told what to do and work to a strict schedule; this is particularly true when people have a highly complex and demanding life outside work, leaving them little energy or desire to take on additional responsibility in their jobs. However, they are not likely to be high achievers.

Dinah noticed that her new secretary, who had seemed very keen on the job at first, was performing less and less well as time went on. She was making mistakes in simple letters, had been abrupt on the telephone with several of the senior consultants, took long lunch 'hours' and had been off sick for a day or two at a time on several occasions. On taking her to task about all this, Dinah discovered that the woman was bored with the job. 'There's lots of things I could do which you do yourself,' she complained, 'for example, you don't need to dictate every letter – just tell me what you want to say and I'll compose it. And I can organize your diary for you so that you don't book two meetings at the same time – I get the blame for that anyway. I can set up your meetings as well, and contact the other people.'

How much freedom over the way they do their jobs do you give your staff? Could you give them more responsibility – more autonomy over what they do?

Feedback

People need to know whether they are performing their jobs satisfactorily; they need praise for doing things well and they need help and advice if they are not performing up to standard. This may – and usually should – involve you in giving individual feedback to your staff, but other performance measures such as quality checks, formal appraisal and performance reviews can be used for this purpose. However, praise and/or criticism should, ideally, be given as close to the event as possible. It is not much use saying 'By the way, you did a really good job on that account' six months after it happened, particularly to a new employee. The person might have experienced a sense of intrinsic achievement in doing a good job; how much better that sense of achievement would have been if it had had someone else's recognition.

Although Hackman and Oldham's job characteristics were developed more than 20 years ago, they are still recognized as being of value today. Unfortunately, not enough jobs contain all the characteristics and there is nearly always room for improvement.

DESIGNING OR REDESIGNING THE JOBS OF YOUR STAFF

Very few of us get the chance to design jobs from scratch; sometimes you may be lucky enough to be involved in drawing up job descriptions or specifications for new jobs created as a result of growth or the introduction of new technology. And, of course, you can use the opportunity created by recruitment to redefine an existing job.

Designing the job itself is one part of the process; the other is matching the right person to the right job so that the degree of skill variety, task identity and task significance matches the needs and abilities of the individual. There are, however, a number of ways in which some of the characteristics identified by Hackman and Oldham can be improved, including:

- job rotation (increasing skill variety);
- job enrichment (increasing responsibility and thus task identity and significance and autonomy);
- autonomous working groups (increasing autonomy);
- quality circles (increasing job satisfaction).

Job rotation

Job rotation is one way of increasing skill variety as well as being a method of introducing new employees to a wider area than their own job. It is a form of internal job transfer and can reduce the boredom and monotony associated with repetitive, low-level jobs. Its benefits however, are limited in making any lasting contribution to job satisfaction.

Job enrichment

Job enrichment (sometimes called job enhancement) can be very effective in increasing satisfaction providing it is aimed specifically at increasing the level of responsibility of the individual. It should not be confused with 'job enlargement' which too often means just giving the employee more work of the same type.

In five years, Bausch and Lomb, the factory in Waterford where Ray-Ban sunglasses are made, changed from a traditional assembly line with standard job evaluation and grading to a new, cellular system based on teams. Before the change, members of the design team toured the factory, interviewing employees. They asked each person whether they liked their job, how it could be improved and, specifically, whether they would like a wider range of tasks and more responsibility. The answer was an overwhelming 'Yes.'

Autonomous working groups

Increased responsibility and autonomy can also be provided by team working where the team is responsible for work allocation and organization. The construction industry is a good example of this where work is sub-contracted to teams of workers. These working groups can also provide opportunities for increased skill variety and opportunities for more flexible working and individual development.

Additionally, they provide social companionship and a sense of pride in the team's work. Not all teams are effective, however, and conflict may arise between team members, particularly if there is individual competition for different tasks; there is also the need for team leaders to be trained in the skills of leadership and supervision if they are to take over the duties of work organization.

Quality circles

The introduction of the ideas of Total Quality Management and programmes of continuous quality improvement have brought with them a commitment to employee involvement in all aspects of quality, including the setting up of 'quality circles'. These circles are usually set up to tackle a particular project where quality improvement is necessary.

To be successful, quality improvement programmes need commitment from top management; this means not only looking at quality control systems and rewarding individuals and teams for improved quality, but actively encouraging participation through providing time and training.

Bill worked in the Development Services Department of ICL. With his colleagues, he formed a quality circle to tackle problems associated with their work. In this case, it involved the transportation and handling of small electronic components. The group were given time off to hold their meetings and a room in which to meet. Their success in solving the problem was rewarded by a cheque for £1,000. Bill himself felt he had benefited from the project by learning more about working with and managing other people in the quality circle.

Quality circles are more successful when they are coping with issues that affect the jobs of their members rather than with more general and ambiguous problems. They can contribute to job satisfaction through the sense of achievement their members feel when quality is improved and through recognition of their work.

Investigate Could any of the above ideas be put into practice in your area of responsibility to increase job satisfaction?

ALTERNATIVE METHODS OF ORGANIZING WORK

Since the traditional 'job for life' concept has virtually disappeared and the widespread introduction of new technology has had a major impact on job design, there is an increasing opportunity to survey normal working practices and see whether these could be changed.

Flexible working hours, job sharing, home working, adaptation of work methods for people with disabilities are some of the more enterprising ways of work organization. They are not without their problems nor, in some cases, without high initial costs, but they can all bring benefits if well managed. In examining these possibilities, as indeed with job design more generally, consideration must be given to health and safety at work, which is discussed in more detail in Chapter 10.

Flexible working hours

Many organizations already operate embryonic flexible working hours but few have looked into all the opportunities which are available. Flexibility in working arrangements is attractive to employees and can contribute significantly to job satisfaction. The organization can benefit from lower absenteeism, better timekeeping, reduced staff turnover, higher work commitment and improved performance; employees see the advantages of more leisure time, less time spent commuting at peak times, increased responsibility and the ability to schedule work and personal life to the individual's satisfaction.

Flexible working hours can range from a daily, fixed-but-flexible starting and finishing time to the working day to a system of annualized hours over a full year. Employees may work any eight consecutive hours, for example, between 7.30 a.m. and 6.30 p.m. This has the added advantage in providing maximum cover for essential operations such as telephone enquiries or emergencies over a longer period than the typical 9–5 working day. Or they may work a given number of hours during a working week or fortnight, some of which is designated as 'core time' (when staff are required to be at their place of work) and the rest as 'flexible time'. This flexible time might account, for example, for four hours of any working day; in agreement with the manager, the employee can select which particular four hours he or she will work for the rest of each day.

However, annualized hours systems involve a great deal of management time to set up, agree and implement. One of its undoubted benefits is the ability to roster employees to work more and longer hours during peak times and fewer, shorter hours during slack periods.

Compressed working week

This arrangement allows employees to work longer than normal hours for part of a week and have the rest of the time free. It is another variation of flexible working hours but can result in increased fatigue at work, concern and resistance from unions and increases the chance of employees taking on 'second jobs' during their free time, thus reducing commitment and increasing fatigue.

Job sharing

With job sharing, two part-time employees split one full-time job; the salary and hours of work are usually split equally but there is also room for unequal shares. This can benefit people with childcare or other dependant commitments, people who tire easily or have physical limitations, people who want to indulge in part-time study and older people who want to phase-in their retirement. Providing the two job sharers communicate fully with each other, this arrangement can work well, but continuity is essential.

Career-break schemes

Although not defined as an alternative working method, organizations which make provisions for employees to take career breaks while retaining their right to return to work at a later date, usually benefit from such schemes. They are normally aimed at women or men who want to take time at home to be with young children but they can also be used for employees who want time off to study full-time or to experience working practice elsewhere.

Barclays Bank have experienced a big increase in the number of women returning to work after maternity leave after introducing its career-break scheme. There is now an option open to women in senior grades to take a long break or return to work part-time for a period of two years in their existing grade. Providing they work at least 14 hours a week, part-time women in the scheme continue to receive pro rata all the benefits of full-time work, including pensions. Since the scheme was introduced, Barclays has increased its retention of women workers by one-third.

Several companies, particularly in Scandinavia and other parts of mainland Europe, operate local childminding schemes which enable women to return to work. In the UK, Allied Dunbar, Glaxo and East Sussex County Council are among organizations which offer this service. It involves setting up a network of trained childminders and, in some cases, providing the necessary training, who are then matched with employees who wish to take advantage of the scheme.

With the need to recruit and retain more women in the workforce, career-break schemes make good sense to enterprising employers.

Working from home

Although considerable potential savings in rents, heat, lighting and travel could be made if more people worked from home, this is still regarded with suspicion by many employers. There is a feeling of lack of control – but it may merely be a lack of trust in subordinates. Advances in technology and reductions in its cost make it a sensible option to consider.

Oxfordshire County Council have introduced a 'flexiplace' project which gives staff greater flexibility over where and when they work. For example, Jan, a management accountant, works 10 hours of her 30-hour week at home. Office time is used for meetings and face-to-face communication; at home, she works on spreadsheets on her computer. This fits in well with her home commitments; she tries to work in the office during school hours and at home in the evening. In this way, she can spend a satisfying amount of time each day with her family. Alice, whose job as an Education Adviser involves considerable travelling around the County, has a child of school age but opts to work from home most of the time even though her daughter does not require home-based child care: she goes into the office for meetings but finds it easier to fit in her other commitments by travelling to and from her home.

Jobs that involve a great deal of computer-based work can readily be done from home. Employers provide fax machines, mobile phones, answering machines, pagers and laptop computers needed for home-based employees to keep in touch with colleagues and clients. People whose work involves a lot of travelling such as social workers and sales staff can also use their home as a base rather than take up office space which is left empty most of the time.

> IBM sales staff and others who spend much of their time away from the workplace are now provided with mobile telephones and laptop computers in the creation of the 'deskless office'. In the workplace, desks are shared between two or more employees who work in sales, client support, servicing and engineering in IBM's London and Glasgow offices. A similar system is operated in the offices of Coopers and Lybrand Deloitte whereby consultants who need to work in the office when they are not out meeting clients are allocated part of a filing cabinet. They work at any available desk, letting the switchboard know on which telephone extension they can be reached that day.

Not everyone wants to work from or at home. Many people enjoy the social life they find at work and not all home environments are suitable for working in. The loss of social interaction, 'corridor conversations' and knowing what is going on can lower an employee's interest in and commitment to the organization.

Summary

In this chapter we have looked at your relations as a manager with individuals in the organization. The word 'individual' is important since it signals the differences in behaviour, ability and experience of those who work with, and for, you. It also indicates that different people will value different rewards from the work they do.

The work of Maslow and Herzberg helps us to understand the disparate needs that individuals have and what benefits they value in terms of job satisfaction and motivation to work. Herzberg also identifies factors which lead to below-average performance and suggests that the removal or improvement of these factors will reduce dissatisfaction. Expectancy Theory is important in that it examines the strength of the links between effort, performance and rewards and how these affect job satisfaction. The particular role of pay in increasing or decreasing motivation is considered since it is the most common variant open to organizations and managers. In fact, the level of pay is not seen as having motivational impact but can be a source of dissatisfaction.

Changing the design of jobs can increase job satisfaction and benefit individuals, management and the organization as a whole. Well-designed jobs are characterized by the amount of skill variety, task identity, task significance, autonomy and feedback they involve. Job satisfaction can be increased through methods such as job rotation, job enrichment, the creation of autonomous working groups and quality circles.

Another way of reorganizing work is to consider changes in working hours and practices, including the introduction of flexible working hours, job sharing and home working. Finally, whatever the job and however it is designed, you as a manager need to be familiar with the main provisions of the Health and Safety at Work Act in order to provide a safe working environment, and this is briefly outlined in Chapter 10.

Activities

1 How could you increase the motivation of your staff? Can you:
    (a) Increase job 'satisfiers'?
    (b) Decrease 'dissatisfiers'?

2 Which of the following ways of improving job satisfaction for your staff might you be able to introduce?
- Job rotation
- Job enrichment
- Increasing autonomy
- Creating quality circles

3 Which of the jobs carried out in your area of responsibility could be adapted to:
- flexible working hours
- compressed working week
- job sharing
- partial or complete home-based work?

CHAPTER 6

Managing people in groups

INTRODUCTION

Having accepted that there is a range of reasons why people behave differently in a work situation and that you cannot make wild and generalized assumptions about any individual's reasons for performing better or worse than average, you will recognize that when you put individuals together into a group, the behaviour of that group is likely to be unpredictable. Managers spend up to 80 per cent of their time in meetings, many of which constitute working groups, so it is important that they understand about the behaviour of groups.

In this chapter, we will be examining:

- People's behaviour in groups.
- The purposes of work groups.
- Informal groups at work.
- The stages of group formation.
- Group dynamics.
- What makes work groups perform effectively.

This theme of working in groups will be continued in Chapter 7 when we look at building and leading teams.

PEOPLE'S BEHAVIOUR IN GROUPS

In most organizations, people work in groups at some time or another – in committees, in project teams, or on working parties. In some cases, work is always undertaken by small groups and people rarely work on their own; in other words, the task determines the working practice. This is usually because the task is relatively complex and requires the combined abilities of a number of people or because it involves cooperation between a number of individuals. Organizations themselves tend to be run by small senior management teams today rather than by large boards or by individuals. This is partly because large groups are not as effective at responsive decision-making as smaller ones of around five to seven members and partly because organizations are faced with a massive amount of complex decision-making. There is also a tendency to believe that power in organizations should be shared rather than being in the hands of one person. However, the prevalent practice of working in small groups is not always entirely successful.

In common with many organizations, Shell UK adopted a policy of decentralizing its decision-making in the late 1980s, giving more responsibility to small groups in its business units. As a consequence, the company found that communication suffered and the units became cut off from each other and from the expertise at the centre: the quality of decision-making suffered, resulting in over-runs on some major projects and a deterioration in operational reliability. The company was forced to reconsider its policy.

A strong group is also usually more powerful than a sole individual and can have a considerable effect on organizational policy and practice. This can be seen in the political arena where pressure groups can affect government policy – for example, environmental pressure groups have had a strong effect on the government's attitude towards pollution and health. In the case of a management buy-out by a group of employees, organizations have often taken on a fresh life and become much more successful than before.

A great deal of psychological research has been undertaken on the way people's behaviour changes when they become part of a group. There is, for example, a great pressure for people to conform to the accepted behaviour of the group – known as 'group norms'. Permanent work groups, where membership only changes when someone leaves the group or a new member enters it, develop norms over a long period which become quite rigid; temporary work groups, however, will not develop such stringent norms.

Group norms include the kind of behaviour which is acceptable to the members of the group, such as the degree of formality of its meetings, the way it divides up its work, the leadership style adopted and so on. At the level of detail, group norms can include the way people dress, how they use equipment, attitudes to safety regulations, where each person sits, when rest periods are taken etc. As long as all its members conform to these unwritten 'rules', the group will be a close-knit entity which resists change to its working practices, although this does not necessarily mean it is particularly effective. Group members who do not conform are regarded with suspicion and pressure is put on them by others to modify their behaviour so that they 'fit in'.

When Mike was invited to join the Computer Implementation Group he was delighted that he would now have the opportunity to influence the company's policy on new computer systems. He spoke eloquently and at length on his vision for the future at his first meeting and was satisfied that he had made a number of important points. However, when he read the minutes of the meeting, he saw that this contribution had been relegated to a few lines whereas the main business appeared to have been the need for new security precautions, even though this had been agreed months earlier.

He confided his bewilderment to another member of the group who said 'But that's the way things happen here. What you said was interesting – although you took far too long about it; no one ever speaks for more than a few minutes at these meetings. You're very new to all this. Wait a bit before you come in with all these new ideas and then only one at a time.'

Mike would not believe him and tried again; he was politely ignored by the other members who were trying to get to grips with some system for improving internal mail sorting. Eventually, he took the other person's advice and kept quiet for a few months. When he eventually put forward his idea for changing the program the company used for its annual budgeting exercise, he was taken more seriously – he had 'conformed' and the group was prepared, at least, to listen to what he had to say.

There are trade-offs in being a member of a group. You may have to conform to behaviour which, as an individual, you are not used to or find difficult. However, your acceptance by such a group will depend on the extent to which you conform to its norms. If you do conform, you will be accepted as a group member and share fully in its activities.

Groups often rely on consensus in making decisions. Not everyone may agree individually on which way the decision should go, but will agree with the majority. Consensus decision-making is usually effective in that all the individual members of the group have had a chance to air their views and to listen to the views of colleagues; if the eventual decision is agreed by the majority and the minority accept it, it is usually sound. Unless, of course, the group has reached the stage of 'groupthink'.

The phenomenon of 'groupthink', identified by Janis (1982), tends to occur when a group has been formed for some considerable time, there is strong group pressure and there is over-confidence by its members in the group's power and influence. There is a marked deterioration in the group's efficiency and it tends to believe in its own morality – it thinks it is indispensable and invincible, and always right. As a result, it considers any decision it makes, good or bad, will be the correct one and gives up evaluating the quality of the decisions it makes. This can become a very dangerous situation if the group is powerful.

THE PURPOSES OF WORK GROUPS

Organizations create formal work groups for a number of reasons. Charles Handy (1993) identifies the following:

- for the distribution of work;
- for the management and control of work;
- for problem-solving and decision-making;
- for processing information;
- for testing and ratifying decisions;
- for coordination and liaison;
- for increasing commitment and involvement;
- for negotiation and conflict resolution;
- for inquest or enquiry into the past.

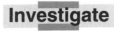 **Investigate**   Think of any work group of which you are a member and, from the above list, try to identify its purpose(s).

Sometimes, groups try to fulfil more than one function or overflow from one function to another. For example, if a group has been successful in problem-solving and decision-making, it might be asked to carry out the tasks of negotiation and conflict resolution associated with the decisions it has reached. However, this may be short-sighted. The same group may not be so successful in its second purpose simply because it was successful in its first.

The kinds of groups which carry out the functions suggested by Handy are nearly always formally created and constituted by the organization. In this way, they have organizational authority to perform their stated function (but not, necessarily, to carry out other associated functions). Informal or interest groups also exist in organizations as you will see in the next section.

People belong to groups for a number of reasons. One reason for belonging to a group is the satisfaction of what Maslow defined as 'social needs' and, indeed, what Herzberg identified as a desire to be recognized (see Chapter 5); people can define their identity through their membership of certain groups. People belong to local political or pressure groups, for example, because they experience a shared set of values with the other people in the group which reinforces their own values.

At work, however, they may be asked, or told, to join a certain work group because of particular knowledge or experience in some area which is necessary to the group's performance; they may represent some staff category or other organizational purpose; they may have certain power within the organization and be able to get things done. Their original purpose for being in the group may have nothing to do with their social needs and they may feel alienated amongst people whose values are different from their own and in line with the particular norms of the group. The group, however, must have a shared purpose, which needs to be clearly identified if the organization expects everyone in it to work towards the same objectives.

Safeway, the retail foodstore chain, has a clear mission statement which is included in each member of staff's job description. It permeates the company and work groups are clear that whatever they are asked to do, or choose to do, must fulfil the same purpose.

Investigate

Think of any formal work group of which you are a member. Does it have clear objectives which are understood and shared by all its members? How do these objectives relate to the overall objective or mission statement of your organization?

INFORMAL GROUPS AT WORK

Organizations also breed informal groups which spring up despite, and sometimes in opposition to, the organization. These may be formed by people who share a common problem at work or dissatisfaction with working conditions. For this reason they are often referred to as 'interest' groups since the members of the group share a common interest in work-related matters. They may be formed through some shared concern such as a desire for equal opportunities practices at work or the perceived need for a staff canteen or a non-smoking policy. Or they may be groups of people with shared interests and beliefs outside their work context – for example in voluntary work, amateur dramatics or a particular religion. These groups have no authority in the eyes of the organization, although they can satisfy social needs and may create considerable pressure for change.

The kinds of issues which give rise to the formation of interest groups include the following, identified by Professor Sandra Dawson of The Judge Institute, Cambridge University (Dawson, 1992):

- The division of organizational profit between different groups associated with the organization.
- How pay increases or promotion are secured.
- How to avoid redundancy and gain job security.
- How people are treated by their bosses.
- What is a 'good' job.
- How different functions in the organization should link together and what is their relative importance.
- The amount of 'discretion' or 'control' over different jobs.
- The way the organization should be going.

These are the kinds of issues which can be the subject of converzation amongst employees over lunch or during a coffee break – the core of 'corridor converzations'. Often, the people who take part in them do not see themselves as a member of an informal or interest group – they see the issues as matters of common concern. Yet, not always does everyone share this concern; in some cases, one person may sympathize with another over a particular issue but have no personal interest in it themselves. As you will see in Chapter 9, a group of people who share a common grievance can make more impact than a single individual.

A college was attempting to change its organizational structure. Currently, it was run by the Principal and two Deputy Principals with other staff taking on informal roles in staff development, curriculum and course design and student counselling. It was generally agreed that the Principal's role was too demanding of a single person and that the roles of the Deputy Principals were unclear and ill-defined. It was also recognized by some staff that the changes in higher education meant an increase in competitiveness and a need for some overt marketing which would increase and change the roles of the existing senior staff.

A small group was set up to look at reorganizing the structure of the college, consisting of a number of people who had expressed considerable interest in this. They followed all the 'rules' for group effectiveness, particularly in communicating their discussions to everyone else. Yet they were disappointed that many of the staff showed little interest in what was going on; they were reasonably happy with the existing structure and either saw no reason to change it or said they would accept any changes that were proposed.

At the same time, the secretarial staff of the college were involved in re-defining their jobs. No formal grouping was set up, yet every member of secretarial and clerical staff took a deep interest in what was going on.

Interest groups may become semi-formalized, as in the first group in the example above, or they may have no real grouping, not even on an informal basis. In some cases, they may exist because people in organizations have professional knowledge and values in common, such as men and women who have trained as engineers or as personnel specialists. These individuals have already shared in a specific and lengthy training, with restricted entry and a commitment to a distinct body of specialized knowledge which gives them a shared interest (Dawson, 1992).

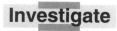
Investigate

Do any interest groups exist in your organization? Are they semi-formal, informal or unformed?

THE STAGES OF GROUP FORMATION

Before a group can perform effectively, it needs to go through a number of stages. Four of these are identified by Tuckman (1965) as:

■ Forming
■ Storming
■ Norming
■ Performing

To these, we could add a fifth stage:

■ Mourning

Forming

This is the initial, testing stage when the group comes together for the first few meetings. At this stage, the group is merely a collection of individuals, each with personal ideas and agendas, wanting to see how they will 'fit in' and what the other members of the group are like.

Typical behaviour at this point will be wary; individuals will be polite to each other and somewhat guarded in what they say or agree to do. They will probably not divulge anything about themselves unless asked to do so. They will be assessing the group leader – is he or she likely to be formal or informal, directive or consultative? What kind of authority has the leader got? There will be a considerable amount of silence as people weigh each other up and most of the discussion will probably be concerned with structure – what the group is going to do, how work will be divided up, what are the objectives of the task.

One way of helping to reduce anxiety at this stage is for the group to undergo some kind of 'ice-breaking' exercise. This could take the form of each person interviewing another and then 'introducing' that person to the rest of the group. Certainly, name cards are helpful at this stage when people often do not know the names of the other members of the group.

Storming

The second stage of group formation is characterized by conflict, which may be open or hidden. Although, in the initial stage, agreement may appear to have been reached about group objectives, leadership, roles etc., these may be challenged in the second stage. Individual members may start to test their strength. This may take the form of outright confrontation such as 'What right do you have to say that?' or 'I didn't agree with her ideas at the time and I still don't.'

Or people may simply opt out and refuse to take part in discussion or work with other people. Sub-groups are likely to form – there is strength in alliances and people often feel happier if they can share their feelings and grievances with other sympathetic members of the group.

The group can feel it is not getting anywhere during this storming phase, which is depressing for its members, and it can even degenerate into a noisy and rebellious band of squabbling and in-fighting individuals. This, however, is the worst scenario and most people realize that it is unproductive. It is usually better for the leader of the group – or one or more of its members – to bring the conflict out into the open and try to discuss it. In reality, this often means going back to the first stage and re-defining the objectives and roles of the group. If this is successful, members of the group will develop trust in each other which is essential to the group's working successfully.

Norming

At this stage, once the group is clear about what it is going to do and has passed through the earlier stages, it can begin to get itself organized. By this time, clearer roles are emerging and people are more certain about what they are expected to contribute. This is when the group begins to establish procedures and group norms and when individuals test the working of the group and determine their levels of commitment to it.

It is a period when, providing trust has been established, people can confront issues and give constructive feedback to each other. People will begin to talk more openly and learn to listen to the views of others. Even when these views conflict with their own, they will be prepared to give them serious consideration. The group is moving towards solidarity.

Performing

This stage will only be reached when the other three stages have been completed successfully; some groups never reach it. The individual members of the group will have established rapport with others, making allowances for weaknesses and building on individual and group strengths. There will be both an open atmosphere in which problems and ideas can be talked about and resolved without conflict and a close, supportive ambience with which individuals feel comfortable –

a sense of 'belonging'. By the time the group reaches this stage, it is at its most productive.

Mourning

The word 'mourning' denotes the breaking up of a successful group – group members 'mourn' the loss of the support and group identity they had valued. However, it should also be a time of remembering what went on in the group and what made it so successful – a period of evaluation from which everyone can learn something about being a group member. Too often, the memory of a highly successful group acquires a kind of aura which clouds the recollection of its less successful functioning – particularly of the 'storming' phase. Ideally, everyone needs to learn from each experience of working in a group so that they can increase their personal effectiveness as a group member.

Not all stages will take the same length of time. For a group whose members already know each other and where the task is relatively simple and highly defined, such as 'Produce an outline induction and training programme for new staff in the Department', the first three stages may be dealt with in a few hours. For a more complex task, with low definition and where people are coming together in a group for the first time (such as in a project team), you should expect the stages to take considerably longer.

GROUP DYNAMICS

Organizations which run training courses for managers and others outside the organization are able to introduce the idea of group dynamics in a realistic way. For a period of time, usually about a week, people from different organizations and working backgrounds are thrown together to work intensively in small groups, analysing and solving problems and reaching decisions. Part of this time is often spent in reflecting on the way in which the group is behaving – the process of group dynamics rather than the content of the task it has been set.

This may sound like contemplation of one's own navel, but it is usually a very rewarding aspect of these kinds of training courses. It has to be handled sensitively, of course, since people are likely to discover things about themselves which they would rather not know. However, this is not so threatening in a situation where they will not be working with the others in this group again, or even in the same organization.

The previous section outlined the stages a group goes through when it takes on a task. This can be used as the basis for looking at how the group is behaving at any time during its formation. Group dynamics, however, also focuses on the individual – how he or she is behaving, how he or she relates to other members of the group, what any person is contributing, whether individuals are seeking power or are opting out or whether some group members are being deliberately or unwittingly excluded. The essential ingredient for examining group dynamics is trust between its members so that anyone can speak openly about their feelings and reactions.

The task the group is undertaking usually assumes prime importance, particularly when groups are competing with each other on the same task as happens on training courses. It happens in organizations too, when different project teams are competing for additional resources or individuals are seeking rewards. In particular, ambitious and confident people can run away with the task without realizing that what they are doing is not necessarily the only, or best way, of tackling it. Since they do not listen to others in the group, they are not using the potential resources which a group of people brings to any problem.

Sue was a very high-powered Chief Executive in a small company and expected to adopt the leadership of any group she worked in. However, working with other senior people outside her organization, she discovered that she was in competition for leadership of the group. At first she tried to assert herself by being aggressive and, when that failed, decided she would have nothing further to do with the group. During discussions, she had to come to terms with the fact that she was a fairly large fish in a rather small pond in her own organization and lacked some essential leadership skills.

Sam was a member of a group of 12 people, working on a problem-solving exercise. He felt his ideas were ignored and that nobody listened to him. He confided in the group leader that he suspected racial discrimination since everyone else in the group was white. At a group meeting, he discovered that three other people felt exactly the same way as he did, in that they also felt excluded, and it was agreed that the group was too large to function effectively and that it would work as two sub-groups in future. Sam agreed that the problem was one of size rather than of colour or race.

Group effectiveness

There are a large number of factors which interact to determine how effective – or ineffective – a group may be. These include:

- The size of the group.
- Group membership characteristics.
- The stages of its development.
- The task the group has to undertake.
- The kind of organization in which the group is working.
- The group leader.
- Group processes and procedures.
- Group communication.

With the exception of the stages a group passes through, which were covered earlier, we will look at each of these in turn.

The size of the group

The optimum size of a work group is between five and seven members. This size of group allows everyone to participate more or less equally and to get to know each other reasonably well. Once the group becomes larger, participation and communication become more problematic.

Yet some groups need to be larger because the task requires a number of specialists or because widespread representation is thought to be essential. In these cases, it is usually better to divide the group into sub-groups, each with its own responsibilities, meeting as a large group only when it is necessary. Committees, for example, which are often too large because of the need for representation from a number of different parts of the organization, usually operate more effectively when Working Parties or Task Forces are formed from amongst the members for specific tasks. Groups with over 20 members which do not break down into sub-groups tend to suffer from absenteeism and low morale.

Group membership characteristics

Although people who think and act in similar ways may feel happier working in a group together, this is not always a recipe for success. A mix of skills and characteristics is necessary for a group to be effective.

In the next chapter, we will be looking at the kinds of roles people can adopt in groups and how the mix of roles contributes to the group's success. At this stage, however, it is important to recognize that many groups are determined by the individual's role in the organization – manager, charge-hand, union representative and so on. Although these hierarchical roles may determine who belongs to a particular work group, the individual's role in that group may not be the same as the title he or she possesses in organizational terms.

The task the group has to undertake

People are brought together into work groups because there is a particular task which the organization has identified as needing to be undertaken. These tasks relate back to Handy's purposes of work groups and might include problem-solving, idea generation, planning and implementing change, quality improvement, decision-making, policy formation, procedural definition etc. The type of task will determine who belongs to the group. For example, how many and which specialists or experts are needed, which parts of the organization need to be represented.

The timescale of the task is also an important factor. If the job needs to be completed urgently, a highly structured group with an authoritative leader may be acceptable. Where there is less pressure of time and creative ideas are sought, this is likely to be less acceptable.

The kind of organization in which the group is working

Organizations have their own norms about the way in which things are done and this will be reflected in their work groups. A very bureaucratic organization, for example, such as the Civil Service or the Army, will have procedures for almost any task that needs a work group, even down to who should be members of certain groups. In such circumstances the position of the group leader in the organization's hierarchy is likely to be unchallenged in the work group.

The group leader

As you will have realized, the person who is responsible for leading any group is likely to contribute considerably to the group's success or failure. In some organizations, as we have pointed out, the group leader will have the authority of his or her position in that organization's hierarchy. In other, less highly structured organizations, the leader may lack any recognizable organizational power but may lead the group because they have particular expertise or knowledge which other members of the group lack. Another reason for the choice of a particular person as leader is that they are responsible for and control the group's budget – in this case, 'money is power'. However, even when a formal leader has been appointed from outside or from within the group in its initial 'forming' stage', other people may assume this role. If the leader is poor, unable to encourage the group to get on with its task or to deal with conflict between individual group members, the group is not likely to be very effective. Another person may take over the leadership or this role may be shared by a number of people depending on the task. For example, someone who is knowledgeable about budgeting could assume leadership when decisions need to be made about costing or expenditure; someone else, with a knowledge of personnel procedures, might take on the role where matters relating to staff recruitment, deployment or downsizing are concerned.

Group processes and procedures

These refer to the way in which the group conducts itself in performing its tasks and looking after its members. One model of group process which is effective in approaching a problem-solving task systematically involves going through six steps.

First, the problem needs to be identified and described, preferably as clearly as possible by the person who has recognized it. If it is a problem which the group has been asked to tackle from outside, it still needs to be defined by the group so that everyone understands exactly what it is. This involves the second step, seeking information which will clarify the group's understanding of the problem, often from outside the group. This leads to the third stage – diagnosis. The problem has been identified and all the necessary information about it has been acquired; now the group can effectively determine what the real problem is. Once the problem has been diagnosed, opinions can be put forward by individual group members (the fourth step) and these can be evaluated by other members (step five) before a decision (step six) is made. This kind of rational approach to solving problems and making decisions optimizes the contribution of all the members of the group.

Group communication

When people are working together in a group, the way in which they communicate with each other and with people outside the group affects the way in which the group performs.

Within the group, some pattern of communication usually emerges. One individual may take on all the responsibility of communicating with each member of the group, letting everyone know what everyone else is doing, keeping records, collecting and disseminating information. This works well in a small group and means that everyone is aware of what is going on – provided the individual does the job well. An alternative pattern is where communication is passed on from one person to another. This is slow and often unreliable, as communication can be distorted.

A pattern of 'all-channel' communication inside the group is effective for complex problems whereby everyone is in constant communication with everyone else. Again, this works better in smaller groups since, as the size of the group increases, so does the complexity of this kind of communication. There is also a 'breakdown' factor if one or more group members do not communicate with others.

Communicating with others outside the group is often essential, particularly at a time of change. There is a tendency for groups to become very inward-focusing, forgetting about other people, other departments in the wider organization. These others often need to know, and usually want to know, what the group is doing and how it is progressing. This sort of communication may take place in formal reports to a person to whom the group is responsible, or it may take the form of a wider, public relations exercise through a newsletter to other staff.

The group also needs communication from outside; it needs to be aware of what is happening elsewhere in the organization which might affect its own task; it might need to know what other work groups are doing, particularly if their tasks overlap. No work group is an island and it will certainly not be effective if it believes it is.

Summary

In this chapter we have looked at how people behave when they are formed into work groups. Groups can either be formal, in which case they are constituted and recognized by the organization, or informal, in which case they are often not recognized.

Formal groups can have one or more work-related purposes and need to be clear about their objectives. All groups which meet for a particular purpose pass through a number of stages before they are able to perform effectively, although the length of these stages will vary depending on the membership of the group and the task it has been set.

There are a number of factors which affect how well a work group performs. These include the size of a group, its membership, the task(s) it has to perform, the norms of the organization, the way in which it goes about its work and the way in which it communicates between its members and to other people.

Activities

1 Make a list of groups in your organization about which you are aware. Note beside each one (a) its purpose and (b) whether it is formal, informal or an interest group.
2 Take a group of which you are an active member. What stage in its development has this group reached? Has it moved on or is it moving on through all four stages?
3 Using the headings in the last section, try to assess the effectiveness of your main work group and identify how it might become more effective.

CHAPTER 7

Building and leading your team

INTRODUCTION

Following on from what you have learned about the ways people behave in groups, and how groups can be more, or less, effective, this chapter concentrates on the development and improvement of teams.

Although you may have inherited existing teams in your work, or become a member of an existing team yourself, you are likely to become involved in setting up work teams at some time or another. To do this, you will need to identify the skill or competence requirements needed in team members in relation to the demands of the task. Having done this, you need to identify and assess competences in potential team members in the same way as you needed to assess current skills in relation to recruitment and selection of new staff (Chapters 3 and 4).

Having selected the members of your team, you, as manager, need to establish and agree objectives for team development and working. This may involve using project planning and resource allocation techniques, the details of which are beyond the scope of this book. You will also need to define and allocate workload responsibilities and authority within the team and ensure that you give members of your team constructive feedback on their performance.

In order to maximize team performance, you will need to motivate your staff to reach the team's objectives (see Chapter 5) and provide for learning and skill development where necessary.

Managing a team involves establishing good relationships with all its members through genuine consultation and the establishment of clear lines of communication. This involves not only communicating 'outwards' to others – giving instructions, setting deadlines and so on – but being receptive to 'inward' communication from team members and others. Only by doing this can you assess information which is important and appropriate for your team to receive.

You are also likely to lead team meetings and some advice on that will be given here, although full coverage of that subject would require a book of its own.

In this chapter we will be looking at:

- Forming a team.
- Team roles.
- Setting objectives.
- Monitoring and evaluating progress.
- Running team meetings.
- Self-directed teams.
- The benefits of teams.
- Leading a team.

FORMING A TEAM

Mike Woodcock and Dave Francis, in their book *Organization Development through Teambuilding* (1990), state that an effective team will show the following characteristics:

- It will establish and work towards clear objectives.
- It will have open relationships between members.
- It will deal with different viewpoints and gain from debate.
- Members will show a high level of support for each other.
- Personal relationships will be based on personal knowledge and trust.
- People will want to work together and get things done.
- Potentially damaging conflicts will be worked through and resolved.
- Procedures and decision-making processes will be effective.
- Leadership will be skilful and appropriate to the needs of the team.
- It will regularly review its operations and try to learn from experiences.

■ Individuals will be developed and the team will be capable of dealing with strong and weak personalities.

■ Relations with other groups will be cooperative and open.

Mike Woodcock (1989) identifies problems with ineffective teams, which may be due to:

■ Poor selection and recruitment of team members.
■ Confused organization structure.
■ Lack of control of the team by the leader.
■ Poor training of team members.
■ Low motivation.
■ Low creativity in team members.
■ An inappropriate management philosophy.
■ Lack of succession planning and development.
■ Unclear aims.
■ Unfair or inappropriate rewards.
■ Personal stagnation in team members or leader.

Investigate

Think of a team of which you are either the leader or an active member. Using the above lists as a check, identify which characteristics of your team are present and how effective – or ineffective – it is.

This, then, is what you should be aiming for when setting up and developing a team. Your job will be easier if you are able to select team members yourself based on the demands of the task and the skills and competences required to complete it.

In Chapter 3 on recruitment you were introduced to the idea of job descriptions and employee specifications. The same techniques can be used to identify what the team has to carry out and what kinds of people would be necessary in the team. However, as you will see in the next section, you also have to take into account the balance of people in your team and the kinds of characteristics possessed by individuals. Of course, this assumes an ideal situation in which you are free to choose who will be in your team and those you select are both able and willing to be in it. Organizational reality means that you often have to include certain people because of their work role or place in the hierarchy or that the people you want are already committed to other projects or work.

As leader of a new team, you have to analyse the task it is expected to perform and the skills you will need; to do this you will need a form of 'job description' which sets out the requirements of the task. For example, suppose you were asked to set up a team of people to assess different types of computer software and introduce the preferred option into your department or organization. You might draw up a description of the task in the following way:

Objective: To implement the most appropriate software program into … within a period of *x* months at no more than *y* cost [of course, your time scale and budget may not be determined at this stage].

Method
– identify current and forecast software needs of department/ organization
– identify appropriate commercial software packages
– test software packages
– consider design of package if no appropriate commercial package available
– select or design appropriate software
– load software on to hardware
– train staff in use of software
– evaluate implementation

This would only be a very rough, first shot, at defining the team's task. Once the team is set up, you may have to redefine it in the light of more knowledge about what has to be done.

Looking at this rough description, it is obvious that you are going to need people with computing skills and, possibly, with the competence to design custom-made software. But you are also going to need people who can communicate what the team is doing to others outside the team. You will need to identify the current and future needs of people who will be using the new package. These people may be worried about their ability to operate it, particularly if it is very complex and/or specialized; they will need reassurance. You will also need people who are good trainers, not just people who are good operators. You will also need team members who are willing to undertake the rather unexciting work of testing the software packages … and so on.

Your team member 'employee specification' grows by the minute and, from the last chapter, you know that large teams are less effective than small ones. Of course, you can always elect to work in sub-groups but you need to ensure that people who are going to be working together in small groups not only have the required competence but can work together. If possible, you want to reduce the risk of interpersonal conflict within the group.

One way of deciding upon who should join your team is to look at the team role that a person can play quite apart from his or her particular expertise. Belbin, whose work on management teams (1981, 1993) is well known, differentiates between functional roles such as computer analyst, sales manager, accountant and so on, and team roles which relate to an individual's contribution to the effectiveness of the team. By identifying the particular roles team members can play and by recognizing individual strengths and weaknesses in relation to these roles, you can build a well-balanced and effective team.

TEAM ROLES

Belbin investigated mixed management teams over a long period and concluded that any team member could play one or more of the following roles:

- Implementer
- Coordinator
- Shaper
- Plant
- Source Investigator
- Monitor/Evaluator
- Teamworker
- Completer/Finisher
- Specialist

He devised a Self Perception Inventory which can be used by individual team members to determine in which roles they are strongest and in which they are weakest. Each role has positive and negative aspects which it is necessary for the individual and other team members to recognize.

Investigate   Try the Self Perception Inventory in Belbin's book
Management Teams (1991).

Implementer   c/Rene

This person is disciplined, conscientious and aware of external responsibilities such as the need to keep other people informed about what the team is doing. He or she respects established conditions in the organization and one weakness of the role is a degree of rigidity. On the positive side, this person is very practical, trusting and tolerant of other people. The Implementer's strengths lie in putting other people's ideas and plans into operation and carrying out plans which the team have agreed in a systematic and efficient way.

Coordinator   carol

As you might expect, this denotes the ability to lead the team towards its objectives through effective use of team members. The Coordinator is able to recognize individual strengths and weaknesses in other members of the team and ensure that the best use is made of every person's potential. This role has many positive aspects, its main weakness being that a Coordinator is not usually so effective at 'crisis' management; he or she is likely to prefer a participative, consultative style of leadership, carrying all the rest of the team with them. In cases where the team needs to act under pressure and at high speed, the Shaper can take over.

Shaper   c/Rene

Shapers are people who have a strong need for achievement and success. They are highly competitive with an active desire to win – they put life into a team and can drive through change at the expense of popularity. On the negative side, Shapers are often seen as pushy and aggressive and insensitive to the feelings of others.

The Coordinator and Shaper roles are complementary; the former pulls a team together while the latter challenges the status quo and goads other team members into action.

Plant   Alvin

The Plant is the creative member of the team, full of new ideas and ways of doing things and particularly concerned with finding innovative solutions to major issues. They generally have higher than average intelligence. Often, however, they are weak in communicating their ideas to others and can appear to be on a different wavelength; they are also very sensitive to criticism or praise. If a team contains too many people who are strong in this role, they can conflict with each other over ideas.

The name derives from Belbin's experiments in which he 'planted' individuals who scored highly on creativity in psychometric tests into the companies he was studying (Belbin, 1981).

Resource Investigator CAROL

When studying managers who might be classified as 'Plants', Belbin identified another, complementary role – the Resource Investigator. More outgoing and communicative than the Plant, this person gets around, finds out what is going on, meets people and asks relevant questions. This person is often described as 'never being in the office and, if he or she is, always on the telephone'. Resource Investigators are good communicators and negotiators, always ready to explore new opportunities and make new contacts. They are also good at thinking on their feet and getting information. However, they can quickly lose enthusiasm if the task is not stimulating enough for them.

Monitor/Evaluator cy

Although both Plants and Resource Investigators are valued by teams for their ideas and enthusiasm respectively, both can get carried away if there is no Monitor/Evaluator present. This person is serious-minded and judicious, valued for an ability to make shrewd judge-ments and able to debate with a Plant over the latter's ideas. To other team members, the Monitor/Evaluator can appear as rather dry, bor-ing and over-critical, but this role is essential in a team where the decision-making process is complicated and it is difficult to reach consensus; the Monitor/Evaluator can be relied upon to reach the optimum decision.

Teamworker ABn

Teamworkers are diplomatic and perceptive with a strong interest in people. They are good at building on other people's suggestions, improving communications between different members of the team and generally fostering team spirit. They are particularly effective at averting interpersonal conflict and dealing with difficult team members. The Teamworker will let the Plants in the team have their say even if their ideas may appear impractical to others; he or she can draw out the slower but essential Monitor/Evaluator. A team composed of Teamworkers might sound ideal, but they lack the attributes of some of the other roles and members of such a team would spend all their time supporting one another!

Completer/Finisher

So far we have identified team members who represent the aims of the organization, who can lead the team during stable times and in periods of crisis, people who will have ideas, people who communicate well, people who can reach decisions and people who encourage cooperation; the Completer/Finisher is the final ingredient. He or she is the person who has the ability to carry anything through to its conclusion with complete thoroughness. A team may have many brilliant ideas and even reach decisions, but if the agreed action is not carried out, it will fail in its objectives. This person checks on every detail and ensures nothing is overlooked. Completer/Finishers have high standards for themselves and others and may often be intolerant of people who do not share these standards.

Specialist

This is the person with professional expertise in an area valued and needed by the team in order to achieve its objectives. A team may need more than one Specialist at different times in its evolution. For example, a team involved in a building project would need an architect at the design stage and perhaps someone with expertise in the different properties of particular building materials: they might also need expert help on costing, on computer trunking and so on.

Of course, these team roles are stereotypes and individuals are usually strong in one or two aspects and weak in others. The same person can, therefore, perform more than one role in a team; you do not have to have teams of nine people to fulfil all the roles. The important point is that teams which are well-balanced in terms of the roles team members play will be more effective than teams which are imbalanced and where one or more essential team roles are missing.

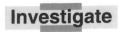 **Investigate**

Imagine that you could form your ideal team. Try to identify people in your organization who would be strong in each of the nine Belbin team roles.

Unfortunately, in real life teams are not always well-balanced. What you should have learned from the discussion of team roles is the reason why some teams are more effective than others. You should be able to recognize the shortcomings in any team of which you are a member.

When you are setting up a team, it is useful to spend some time asking everyone to identify their own strengths and weaknesses and to discuss these with other team members. You could use Belbin's Self Perception Inventory as a starting point. As a result, as a team you will be aware of any general weakness, such as not having anyone whose strength lies in communicating with others or lacking any Plants and thus being short of creative ideas. If you work in a team most of the time, this should also give you some guidance about the kinds of people you need to recruit.

SETTING OBJECTIVES

Just because you are clear about what the team has to achieve – its allotted task – does not necessarily mean that all the members of the team either understand this or necessarily agree with it. Very early in forming a team you need to allocate time to set objectives which everyone is clear about and which can be realistically achieved. The whole team has to be involved in this if you are to get agreement and commitment from everyone and avoid too destructive a 'storming' phase later on.

Alison was asked to head up a team to look at staff development in a small company. She was given a budget for training and three members of staff from different parts of the company to work with her. At their first meeting, she explained their objectives as being to use the budget to provide the maximum amount of essential training within the next 12 months.

At the second meeting she encountered considerable resistance to her ideas although she thought everyone had agreed with what she had said earlier. Tina, from Sales, claimed that most of the budget should be used for training her staff since, unless sales improved, company financial objectives would not be met. John argued strongly for management training to improve performance; Krish insisted that customer service staff badly needed training since they were often the first contact for potential customers. The meeting broke up without anything being agreed and with each member of the team feeling personally aggrieved.

At the next meeting Alison suggested they went back to basics and agree what their objective was in general terms before looking at ways in which they could achieve it.

Organizational objectives are often deliberately vague. At the operational, team level objectives need to be clarified and the team's resources and constraints determined. Once the team has agreed on its overall objectives, the business of putting together an action plan – achieve those objectives is the next step.

In the example above, the team's main constraint was financial, so they went on to look at training options which would not require money, such as in-service training. They identified people in the organization who could contribute to training others and act as mentors to junior staff. They drew up a training plan for each Department within the overall budget and also made recommendations for the budget to be increased in the following year. They also set up ways in which the training and its effectiveness could be monitored and measured and built in a number of review points so that changes to the original action plan could be made in the light of experience.

MONITORING AND EVALUATING PROGRESS

Most teams are drawn together to work over a period of time – anything from a few months to years. One reason for setting objectives is that, over time, the team can check on its progress towards those objectives and, if necessary, make adjustments to the original plan. Things change. Even in a matter of months a team may find that their original plan was too ambitious or that unexpected hitches keep occurring which slow down their progress. Key people may leave the organization and not be replaced immediately, or at all; a sudden crisis may erupt, throwing the team off course; there may be a senior management re-shuffle and priorities may change. Teams can build in 'slack' for unpredictable events and hold-ups but they do not know when or where these will occur. So it is very important for the team to take time at regular, scheduled intervals to check on how it is progressing.

However, setting aside time for review is not particularly productive unless you have some way of measuring progress, and you need to establish some kind of monitoring process early on. Ideally, all objectives should be measurable and you and your team should aim to set out not only what you intend to achieve, but how you can tell whether you have achieved it.

Let us take some objectives and see how they might be measured. For example, a team might have objectives to:

- Reduce production faults by 50 per cent.
- Decrease customer complaints to a minimum.
- Improve staff morale.

The first objective, reducing faults, sounds as if it could be measured, but how much is 50 per cent? You would need at least a base monthly figure of reported faults as a yardstick so that you could check on whether faults were being reduced over the period and that the rate of reduction was being maintained and improved in line with your objective.

And how do you measure customer complaints? Are they all reported or are some anecdotal? You would need to set up a system to record the complaints and probably qualify these as 'serious', 'less serious' and so on. You would then need to monitor the rate of complaints over time to evaluate whether they were decreasing.

The final objective of improving staff morale is much more difficult to measure and should really be avoided at all costs unless you can specify how you will go about this and how you will measure progress. As you saw in Chapter 5, individuals value different rewards and are motivated by different things. There is no 'Staff Morale Improver' which you can buy off the shelf. And how do you measure the improvement? By increased production or better service, by happier people, by less absenteeism, lateness or illness ...?

The main tasks for your team, therefore, in relation to objectives are to:

- Clarify and agree overall objectives.
- Consider options for achieving objectives.
- Set out, step by step, how the team plans to meet their objectives.
- Agree how to measure progress.

- Set a time scale and establish review points.
- Monitor and evaluate progress against measures.
- Adjust plans if necessary.

RUNNING TEAM MEETINGS

The most usual way of communicating between team members is to hold regular meetings. These should also appear in your action plan and should not be held only at review points. Meetings fulfil a number of purposes (Pinder, 1980):

- for making decisions as a team on policy or action;
- to help someone in the team or outside it make a decision;
- to provide support and help for team members or other people;
- to provide information and/or feedback on progress;
- to obtain or pool information;
- to solve a problem;
- to air grievances;
- to throw up new or creative ideas.

Investigate   Think about the last three team meetings you attended. Which of the above purposes did they serve? (They may serve one or more purposes.)

All team meetings should have one or more purposes and, for this reason, should have a written agenda so that everyone knows what they are going to discuss. As the chair of the meeting, you should aim to keep to the agenda so that valuable time is not wasted. It is helpful to everyone not only to state the starting time of the meeting – and keep to it – but to state the finishing time, and keep to that as well.

Someone should keep notes of team meetings which may be circulated afterwards, ideally identifying individuals who agreed to take any kind of action before the next meeting and recording any decisions reached.

The control of the meeting should be with the chair, and this means allowing everyone to put their point of view but not allowing individuals to ramble or overstate their case. Conflict or grievance expressed at meetings can sometimes be dealt with more successfully outside the meeting, involving the participants only.

The place in which you hold meetings is important. Rooms which are too small, too noisy, too hot, too cold, badly ventilated or poorly and uncomfortably furnished will affect people adversely and the meeting is likely to be less successful than if these 'comfort' factors had been attended to. You may combine meetings with lunch – or, as many executives now do, with breakfast – or provide refreshments at the start of the meeting.

People complain about unproductive meetings for a variety of reasons. Some of these include the venue or the time, some relate to short notice about the meeting or not having seen the agenda beforehand; others relate to the lack of notes of earlier meetings, insufficient allowance of time or poor control by the chair. Pinder's rule for meetings is very simple:

> the effective meeting has a valid objective, it is worth holding and it has an effective chairperson.

> The management consultants Hay found that those in outstanding teams were not brighter, more driven or more committed than members of less successful teams but rather these people contributed emotional intelligence – the ability to understand the emotional makeup of others and empathize.

SELF-DIRECTED TEAMS

Self-directed teams are small groups of employees who have day-to-day responsibility for managing themselves and their work. Members typically handle job assignments, plan and schedule work, make production-related decisions and take action on problems with minimal direct supervision. Team members take on many of the tasks that were once reserved for supervisors or managers, including hiring, firing, conducting appraisals and setting schedules (Wellins, 1992).

Self-directed teams can only survive in an organizational culture which encourages empowerment and employee involvement and trust. Team members need to be selected in the same way as individuals but on the basis of their competence at team working, problem identification and solution, coaching and training and job motivation as well as for their technical or specialist skills.

Many managers distrust the idea of self-directed teams, seeing them as eroding the manager's role in controlling and scheduling work, appraising, hiring and firing. Instead, the reality is that because the team assumes most of these functions, the manager takes on an entirely new set of responsibilities including coaching and training team members, serving as a contact point for suppliers, helping teams to gain access to resources and training, filling in when team members are absent or during periods of peak demand and helping teams to co-ordinate with other teams.

Investigate

As a manager, do you think you would like to work in an organization which favours self-directed teams?

THE BENEFITS OF TEAMS

Many of us are so used to working as part of a team that we fail to recognize what benefits accrue from effective teamwork and the dynamism which well-managed teams bring to organizations. As you saw in Chapter 6, people working in groups draw upon each other's strengths to complement individual weaknesses. Team spirit, in itself, can act as a strong motivating force for personal improvement and for loyalty to the employing organization. Working in teams affords the opportunity to develop new areas of competence and different skills, and failure, as well as success, can be shared.

The concept of team roles helps to identify imbalance in groupings of employees and where there are gaps which need to be filled – this knowledge can contribute towards your Human Resource Audit and inform future recruitment, selection and development of staff. Shortfalls in communication can be highlighted both within the team itself and between one team and another, increasing awareness of areas outside its own sphere of responsibility and generating general understanding of the wider organizational context.

LEADING A TEAM

Leadership has become an important issue at organizational and national level in the last few years (James and Burgoyne, 2001). Of course, leadership always has been important since the dawn of history, and in all areas of human activity. Indeed Peter Drucker (1954) has argued that we know no more about it now than was known by ancient Greeks, and that Xenophon's Kyropaidaia is still the best book on the subject. But recently its place in organizational success has been highlighted. There are almost as many theories about leaders and leadership as there are different kinds of people, and any attempt to identify its key attributes is likely to result in a wide range of answers (Mabey and Thomson, 2000). Early research concentrated on trying to identify the personality characteristics of 'good' leaders – and failed. People who were considered to be successful leaders had different characteristics, different levels of intelligence, different skills. Later research looked at the way leaders behaved in different situations, but most experts in the field conclude that leadership cannot be explained just by studying individuals. The leader of a team needs to be related to the task which is being carried out, the needs of the team and the needs of individuals in that team. One useful way of looking at this is to use a simple diagram of interlocking circles (Figure 7.1).

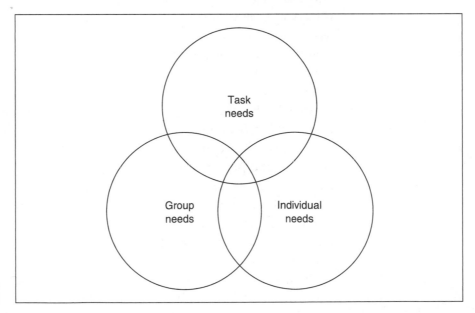

Figure 7.1
The three-circle
model

We start from a rather different perspective than most approaches to leadership, based on three different premises developed by O'Neill (2000). The first of these is that leadership abilities can be developed, and that everyone has some untapped leadership potential. Secondly, O'Neill argues that leadership is diverse, namely that different leadership roles and different situations require different abilities. Thirdly, leadership is distributed, not concentrated at the top; modern organizations need leaders with diverse abilities at every level and in every quarter. O'Neill also argues that there are three main types of leader. First there is the visionary leader, exemplified by those at the top of the organization, whose leadership role is to provide a vision, corporate values, structure and if necessary transform the organization, to ensure organizational survival, and to please the shareholders. Such leaders need a conceptual, 'big picture', externally oriented mindset. At the next level there is the integration leader, as with the head of a department, region or site, whose role is to link the unit into the corporate mission and vision, to develop the unit's system and process infrastructure, and to develop and champion a strong culture and leadership style within the unit, as well as reconciling conflicting interests and goals between units. Here the mindset is medium term, facilitating, boundary spanning, and incorporating corporate values. The third type is that of the fulfilment leader at the project, shift or team level, whose role is to please the customer or client, to deliver operating results on time, to make continuous improvements and increase the productive use of resources. In this context the mindset is short-term, focused on quality and immediate results, with customer service thinking and a human psychology. O'Neill therefore brings leadership down to the level of management which is likely to incorporate your own role.

In an earlier section of this chapter we identified two kinds of people in Belbin's framework who might assume leadership of a team – the Coordinator and the Shaper – depending on the kind of task which the team had been set. Team leadership is not always vested in the person who has been given that position by the organization. It may change hands depending on the situation. For example, there will be times when the team needs to be led by a specialist if it encounters technical or other specialized difficulties; at other times it may be led by someone who has had previous experience of a particular type of problem or project. The best teams profit from the strengths of individual members and recognize when 'leadership' should pass to the most appropriate person. However, someone usually has the responsibility and title of 'team leader', at least in the eyes of the organization, and is accountable for the team's performance.

As was pointed out earlier, the kind of task the team has been set and its time scale will often determine who should lead the team. But the requirements of the task alone are not enough; the team as a group has needs which must be met and individuals within the team have their own needs. People make statements such as 'What we need is leadership' or 'The team needs direction' when they are articulating what the team as a whole feels is lacking. Sometimes teams feel they need support, or feedback, or better communication and they look to the leader for all these things. Within the team, individuals also have their own needs – remember Maslow's hierarchy of needs (Chapter 5). The leader needs to be aware of individual needs and fulfil these as well.

Adair (1983) expanded on the three-circle model by suggesting a number of questions the leader of a team might consider in each of the areas identified in Figure 7.1 when looking at the structure of a team. Adair himself carried out the process shown in Figure 7.2 when performing an 'organization survey' on the Dioceses of York and Chichester as a management consultant.

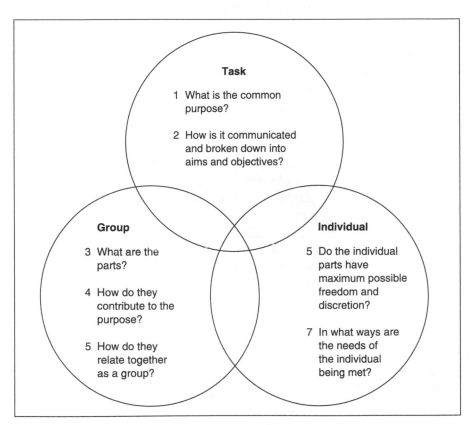

Figure 7.2
Development of the three-circle model of leadership (Adair, 1983)

In summary, a leader has to be all things to all people. He or she has to balance the interrelated demands of the task and the team as well as those of individual team members. This means being directive when it is necessary; giving praise and constructive feedback when people need it; ensuring everyone and everything is operating to its full potential. One final point is the difference between leadership and management; you may well be thinking that much of the above is what being a manager is all about. This is true, but the generally accepted difference is that the role of a leader is primarily in the context of change. With the current rapid rate of change, it is not surprising that there has recently come to be more focus on leadership. Management, on the other hand, is about the organizing and effective operation of a stable, if complex, situation.

Investigate

Think of a team of which you are a member. Does the leader consider the needs of the task, the team and the individual? In which areas is he or she (a) strongest, (b) weakest? Does the three-circle model help you to identify where this person may be lacking in leadership skills?

Summary

Effective teams are characterized by their ability to establish, and work towards, clear goals and by supportive membership, mutual trust, skilful leadership and good relations with other teams and work groups. They depend on effective recruitment, selection and training of team members, high morale and creativity, clear aims and appropriate reward systems.

Although you may not be able to select the particular team members you would wish to have, by evaluating the strengths and weaknesses of existing team members, you can develop a successful team.

Teams need to communicate within the group, and meetings are often the most convenient way of doing this. Meetings should have a recognized purpose, such as reviewing progress, providing information, problem-solving or idea generation. They are costly in terms of time and need to be productive

A recent development has been the rise of self-directed teams, where team members take on many of the functions of managers and supervisors. Such teams, however, can only operate in an organizational culture which encourages empowerment.

Leadership is a very broad concept with a range of different perspectives, but we want to emphasize the approach of distributed leadership. Team leadership is not – and should not be – always vested in an individual by virtue of his or her place in the organizational hierarchy. It may be shared between people with appropriate expertise or abilities and should be determined by the specific needs of the task, the individuals in the team and the team itself. Team leaders are also responsible for ensuring that objectives are clarified, agreed and reviewed frequently. By regular monitoring and evaluation of progress towards agreed objectives, plans can be changed in the light of developments.

Activities

1   For a team of which you are either the leader or an active member, identify its strengths and weaknesses in terms of:
    (a)   its effectiveness;
    (b)   its membership;
    (c)   its leadership.
What can you do about the weaknesses?
2   For a team of which you are the leader or an active member, set out its:
    (a)   general objective;
    (b)   operational plan;
    (c)   measures of progress;
    (d)   systems of monitoring and evaluation of progress.

CHAPTER 8

Managing performance

INTRODUCTION

The growth of performance management has been one of the main developments in HRM in the last decade, although the name itself dates from the 1970s and it is a development from the even older concept of management by objectives. At one level it is strategic in that it is concerned with integrating the different dimensions of an organization's operations; but it is also concerned with the role of the individual manager and indeed expects responsibility to be shared by all members of the organization. The integration is primarily vertical, aligning organizational, team and individual objectives, but can also be functional, bringing together functional strategies in different parts of the organization and within functions, such as integrating different aspects of HRM. We cannot look at all the issues that might be involved in managing performance, but after introducing the principles and measurement of performance, we take up three major components of its operation, appraisal, rewards systems, and the training and development of staff.

In this chapter we will therefore be looking at:

- The principles of performance management.
- Appraisal systems.
- Giving feedback.
- Reward systems.
- Training and developing your staff.
- Methods of development.
- Staff development outside the organization

THE PRINCIPLES OF PERFORMANCE MANAGEMENT

The basic intentions and expectations of performance management are as follows:

- It translates organizational goals into individual, team, and unit goals.
- It helps to clarify the organizational goals.
- It provides a process for measuring outputs compared with objectives but also examines the inputs needed to achieve the objectives.
- It relies on consensus and co-operation rather than control or coercion.
- It encourages self-management of individual performance.
- It is a continuous and evolutionary process, and achieves improvement over time.
- It is strongly associated with development and especially identifying what development is needed.

If all this sounds very attractive, it needs to be noted that it is much harder to implement these principles and achieve the desired outcomes than it is to state them. Fletcher and Williams (1992) in a review of 26 cases of performance management noted 'Aspects of implementation that were weak in some organizations included a rushed pace of change and insufficient training. The better organizations were those which in which there was a more realistic view of development and implementation – two or more years – and in which training dealt with the importance of the line manager's role in coaching and leadership and in managing and providing reward.' Another common reason for difficulty is that schemes are often imposed from above and do not give people, or even middle and junior managers, a sense of ownership in how they develop. Thus McKevitt and Lawton (1996) in studying performance management in the public sector, noted as their central finding 'the lack of attention paid to middle and junior management in the development and implementation of performance measurement systems and hence a lack of embeddedness of systems throughout the organization'. Inadequate account of the prevailing culture is yet another reason for problems. Both of these latter two reasons imply that organizations assume a unitary view, namely that employers and employees share common interests, instead of a pluralist perspective which tries to recognize potential conflicts of interest.

How are performance requirements expressed? Bevan and Thompson (1992) suggest there are five main ways:

- Objectives and targets which define the main outcomes expected.
- Accountabilities for which the individual in question is responsible, such as reaching certain standards.
- Broad responsibilities defined in terms of the key elements of the job.
- Written job descriptions.
- Competences or statements of what the person ought to be able to do.

In considering what measures to use, certain guidelines should be kept in mind:

- They should be output measures not input measures.
- There needs to be a unit of measurement.
- The measures should be objective and observable.
- The results must be within the job holder's control.
- Existing measures should be used where feasible.

It follows that objectives should meet these guidelines, as well as being clear and achievable.

How can performance be measured? The following are some of the main ways in common use:

- Output rating, as with achievement of sales or quality targets or levels of budgeted expenditure.
- Achievement against objectives, in which the manager assesses with the employee the extent which agreed objectives have been achieved.
- Behaviourally based rating scales, which focus on the behaviours rather than the outputs which are desirable for good performance.
- Competences, which are similar to behaviours bur usually broader and in keeping with national or organizational competence standards.
- Critical incidents, in which the focus is key incidents of performance, both positive and negative.

■ Narrative reporting, in which the manager describes the employee's performance in his or her own words.

A different way of looking at measurement is what is measured, as with the following:

■ Financial, as through cost, income, value added, rates of return, shareholder value.
■ Output, such as sales achieved, new accounts opened, units produced.
■ Reaction, such as views of other managers or workers, or clients or customers.
■ Impact, as with changes in behaviour, achievements of given standards, completion of activities, innovative developments.
■ Time, such as speed of response or delivery, turnaround times, levels of backlog.

The issues to be measured ought not to have a single focus, otherwise the employee will tend to concentrate on that to the detriment of other aspects of performance. There has been a move away from ratings, whether single or multiple, to agreed statements that are oriented to behaviour and future improvement. Another trend, although still confined to a relatively small minority of organizations, is towards 360 degree feedback, which involves collecting performance data on individuals from a range of sources, including immediate superiors and subordinates, peers, and both internal and external customers. The concept of the 'balanced scorecard' which brings together customer orientation, financial perspective, internal operational aspects, and innovative or developmental dimensions has become popular at both organizational and lower levels as a result. It also helps to reconcile the competing interests of different stakeholders.

Investigate

How does your organization approach the issues in measuring performance? How do you do it in your own area of responsibility?

Peter knew that he had been lucky to be given the job. The job specification had been just what he had been looking for and it gave him a good outline of his role. But as time went on he realized that something was missing. Although he felt that he was doing a good job, there seemed to be no easy way to demonstrate this, either to his boss or even to himself. He needed some way of measuring himself against the requirements of the job, and he became concerned that his boss didn't seem to have any way of doing this either, so that he began to feel that he was not being properly appreciated.

In a study of 371 hospital employees Alice Gaudine and Alan Saks informed employees about their absence and monitored rates for a year. They found a reduction for employees with a moderately higher than average level of absence but not for those who had high levels of absence.

In conducting a performance review session, it is desirable to have allowed the employee to have engaged in preliminary self-assessment. This involves the employee more directly and is likely to produce a less defensive response. Indeed it is desirable to let the individual do most of the talking, leaving the manager to listen actively for nuances in what is being said, as well as watching for body language. It is also important to recognize achievements. While there are arguments against having forms which must be filled in, thereby adding a bureaucratic element to what should be personal rather than impersonal, a form does help to provide focus and an level of consistency.

APPRAISAL SYSTEMS

Performance management to be effective requires a direct interaction between the management and the workforce, and for most purposes a system of appraisal provides this. There are a number of reasons why appraisal is necessary from the viewpoints of the organization, the manager and the employee.

The organization benefits from:

- standard information about its employees;
- the facility to develop individuals based on appraisal information;
- being able to plan its human resource needs more accurately.

The manager benefits from:

- objective guidelines for assessing staff;
- gaining a better understanding of staff needs;
- improved relationships with staff.

The individual benefits from:

- an opportunity to discuss his or her work objectively;
- the ability to evaluate performance;
- consideration of future training and development needs;
- improved relationships with his or her manager.

Any organization needs to know the strengths and weaknesses of its employees; any manager needs this information about the people who work in his or her department; and any individual needs to know how he or she is performing. A good appraisal scheme can satisfy all these needs. Sir Leonard Peach, former personnel chief at IBM, has suggested that employees should play a larger part in their own appraisal. Amongst his recommendations is that all employees keep a log book which acts as their personnel record. This, he argues, both empowers employees and releases busy managers from some of their responsibilities for appraisal.

You may already operate an appraisal scheme in your organization. If so, this section should help you to assess its current benefits and, if necessary, identify areas for improvement. If, however, you are setting up an appraisal system for the first time, this section will give you some guidelines but you may need to seek professional help from somewhere like the Institute of Personnel and Development or get hold of the advisory booklet on 'Employee Appraisal' from the Advisory, Conciliation and Arbitration Service (ACAS).

An appraisal system helps you as a manager to learn more about your employees, their problems and needs and how their aspirations are being fulfilled by their job. It can help you to increase their motivation by discovering the satisfying and less satisfying aspects of their jobs in the opinion of the individuals who perform them. It can help to improve individual performance and productivity and, thus, increase your job satisfaction as the person accountable for your area of responsibility.

Randell (1984) suggests that an appraisal system should have some – but not, necessarily, all – of the following purposes:

- *Evaluation* – to enable the organization to share out financial and other rewards apparently 'fairly'.
- *Auditing* – to discover the work potential, both present and future, of individuals and departments.

- *Constructing succession plans* – for human resource departmental and corporate planning purposes.
- *Discovering training needs* – by exposing inadequacies and deficiencies that could be remedied through training.
- *Improving standards* – to reach organizational standards and objectives.
- *Developing individuals* – by offering advice, information, praise or sanctions.
- *Improving standards* – and thus performance.
- *Checking the effectiveness* – of personnel procedures and practices.

Investigate

If you currently operate an appraisal system in your organization, which of the above purposes does it fulfil?

If you do not have a formal appraisal system, how do you and your organization fulfil any of the functions above? Is this satisfactory?

In a formal appraisal system, there needs to be an assessment of the individual's performance over a period of time. Self-assessment by the individual is one way of measuring this, as is peer assessment or your own evaluation of how a person is performing in their current job. However, objective measures of performance are preferable and much fairer to the individual. Has he or she achieved an overall, agreed standard of performance against criteria which were known in advance? The job description is an obvious point of reference here, providing it is up to date and, if possible, includes performance measures, or, if the team has set itself objectives which can be measured, the individual can be assessed against these. Unless the individual is actually aware of the standards against which he or she is being measured, the appraisal is unfair and invalid.

Having agreed the objectives and measured the individual against these, that person's strengths and weaknesses in relation to the criteria can be identified. Ideally, these should be set down in writing or on a special appraisal form in agreement with the person being appraised. Thereafter, the appraiser and the person being appraised should discuss and agree (a) what specific training and development the individual needs to remedy weak areas and (b) what his or her objectives should be over the period before the next appraisal or interim review. An interim review is often necessary since most formal appraisals are carried out on an annual basis. Such reviews serve to monitor progress towards the next set of objectives.

The manager needs to establish a relationship of trust with the individual and all appraisal discussions and records should be confidential between those two. In some organizations it is customary for a summary of the appraisal, agreed with the individual, to contribute towards promotion, re-grading or salary review processes: in others, the full appraisal record is used. It is essential, in these cases, that the individual has seen the appraisal summary or report before it goes further.

This contribution to the advancement – or otherwise – of the individual through appraisal has been criticized. The atmosphere of trust between appraiser and appraisee is threatened if not destroyed by the knowledge that a poor appraisal may cost the latter promotion or a salary increase. Some managers hesitate to tell the truth about their subordinates' performance because they dislike upsetting the subordinate or because poor performance may reflect on their own managerial adequacy. In other cases, subordinates may feel considerable dissatisfaction if they do not receive expected rewards and blame their appraiser – rightly or wrongly – for his or her appraisal report.

GIVING FEEDBACK

Although part of the appraisal system will be involved in getting the individual to make a self-appraisal of his or her performance, everyone needs feedback on their performance from others if there is to be any improvement.

We all engage in appraisal on an everyday basis, particularly with people we know well and within our own close domestic circle. We make judgements about whether people are performing above or below our expectations. We comment to others on the performance of the public transport system, the state of the roads, the content of television programmes, the performance of our bosses and subordinates, the way our children behave, the actions of government and the law and so on. Yet, in Western cultures, we hesitate to tell most people about their weaknesses to their faces. And, for many people, it is difficult for them to praise people directly as well.

Giving feedback in an appraisal situation requires sensitivity and openness on the part of the manager. You may have to tell someone that they are not performing well enough and no one likes criticism, even when it is deserved. As the appraiser, you have to be sure that it is not your fault, or the organization's that the person is not performing as well as expected. Not infrequently, the appraisal reveals that lack of essential training or lack of resources and time are contributing significantly to below-average performance.

Gil knew he had a difficult time ahead when it came to appraising Andy. The man just wasn't up to the job and his team were performing less well than any of the others – they never seemed to produce results. He had had to make a presentation to the Board earlier in the year and, by all accounts, it had been disastrous.

Andy was defensive, 'It's all this extra work I'm expected to do,' he complained, 'it doesn't leave me enough time. And everyone else in my team has been here longer than me and knows what they're doing.' Through careful questioning, Gil discovered that the Sales Manager had asked Andy to prepare a detailed sales plan for the department which Gil knew nothing about. He also realized that Andy had not been given any induction when he joined the company and that, when he had asked to be sent on a course to improve his presentation skills, Gil's assistant had turned this down. Much of Andy's poor performance was not his own fault.

Carly was dreading her annual appraisal. She knew that the parents of two of the children in her class had objected formally about how much homework she was giving out and that, despite all her efforts, the end-of-term show had been poorly organized. Her Junior Choir had excelled themselves at the Festival but, on the other hand, class work was a bit behind and she was always late with her reports.

She was pleasantly surprised when Miss Bowles praised her not only about the choir's success but also about her work with two children with learning difficulties, and felt relaxed enough to admit her own shortcomings in other parts of her job. She agreed that she had taken on too much and set her targets too high initially and that she needed to prioritize her work and manage her time better. Together they agreed on her objectives for the following year, with interim objectives which Miss Bowles would review with her at the end of each term. Carly also agreed to attend a time management course which was being run locally – she wished she'd known about this before. She left her appraisal with a sense of relief that they had been able to discuss her weak areas objectively and identify ways of improvement in these and she was buoyed up by the recognition of what she had done well.

'The praise sandwich' has long been a cornerstone of giving feedback – praising the subordinate at the outset for good performance, followed by a constructive discussion of areas of weakness and concluding with a restatement of his or her strengths. An appraisal which concentrates almost solely on areas of poor performance will result in the person being appraised feeling resentful and poorly motivated to improve.

Investigate   When did you last praise someone for their performance at work?

MANAGING REWARDS

Rewards are central to work and are the key quid pro quo which workers receive for their efforts. We have already looked as pay as a motivator in Chapter 4. But it is too easy to think of pay as the main focus of rewards to the exclusion of other aspects of rewards at work, which can be both intrinsic and extrinsic, as noted below:

Intrinsic rewards

- Self-respect
- Sense of achievement
- Feeling of having learned something
- Feeling of having contributed to a team or wider effort
- Self-actualization

Extrinsic rewards

- Pay
- Fringe benefits – holidays, pensions, sick pay etc.
- Pleasant working conditions
- Personal development
- Promotion and career opportunities
- Variety and challenge of work
- Status within organization
- Status outside organization
- Praise
- Friendship

Investigate

How you rank the above rewards in terms of your own priorities? What do you think the priorities of those working for you would be?

Different people will have different attitudes to different parts of the range of rewards. Some people, who are highly instrumental, will want to maximize their direct earnings and little else. Others see pay as secondary to the self-esteem and social opportunities they see work as providing. Others again will focus on non-work aspects of life and want work to interfere with these as little as possible. Workers can also be in quite different situations, with some being in stable, core jobs, and others being in much less stable peripheral positions, and this too will influence their attitudes towards an optimum set of rewards. Employees will see rewards as a key indicator of whether the employer is treating them fairly and transparently in relation both to the work they do and also as compared to other workers. The job of the manager is to understand how different aspects of rewards are valued by the employees, with a view to maximizing both their mix of rewards and the efficiencies which the employer is seeking. But the manager must also cope with individual differences in the valuation of the reward, and also changes over time in way rewards are perceived. Few reward systems are capable of producing optimal results indefinitely, and most need reviewing regularly. This is particularly true of payment systems.

From the company's perspective, it needs to provide rewards that meet a number of objectives:

- Add value to the organization, bearing in mind that personnel costs are typically more than half and often much more than half of total organizational costs.
- Support the main strategic objectives of efficiency, quality, teamwork, and customer orientation.
- Relates to external market factors, but not to the exclusion of internal dimensions.
- Obtain a suitably skilled and efficient labour force.
- Communicate the organization's expectations of performance and standards.
- Is integrated with other HR policies.
- Has some contribution from line managers to permit a devolved implementation of performance management.

- Is comprehensible, equitable and transparent in its operation.
- Encourage appropriate behaviour in relation to the organization's goals.

Rewards are a matter of market as well as performance or job factors. Broadly speaking, the bargaining power of unskilled and semi-skilled workers in the labour market has declined, especially where such skills can be substituted by technology or lower paid workers in other countries. On the other hand, the power of certain types of knowledge workers who hold key aspects of intellectual capital in their heads and can take the assets of the organization with them when they leave the building has increased very considerably. These factors are primarily to do with the nature of external labour markets, but there are also internal factors in which individual contributions can be taken into account. It is also quite possible that collective bargaining with trade unions will be an influential determinant.

Line managers are likely to be involved in some aspects of the reward system, either through job evaluation or some other method of relating one job to another, or through a more direct system of performance-related pay.

TRAINING AND DEVELOPING YOUR STAFF

A survey carried out for Investors in People UK in 1996 showed that today's young people value training and development opportunities over pay and perks. Seventy-three per cent of those surveyed said they would stay with a company that invested time and energy in their development rather than move to a rival that paid more money but was less interested in helping them to progress.

Since the mid-1980s it has been widely recognized that the training and development of staff should be a major item on any organization's agenda. The Chartered Institute of Personnel and Development (CIPD) has drawn up a series of codes of good practice for employers which embody aims, policies and guidelines for implementation; one of these, called Continuous Development: People and Work, states in its introduction:

'continuous development' is self-directed, lifelong learning. Continuous development policies are policies first to allow and then to facilitate such learning at work, through work itself.

It goes on to state that:

'Successful continuous development demands:

- rapid and effective communication of priority operational needs;
- the availability of appropriate learning facilities and resources as a normal part of working life;
- recognition by each employee that he or she shares ownership of any organizational collective learning plan;
- recognition by each employee that he or she is able to create some personal development plan;
- that all strategic and tactical operational plans fully take into account the learning implications for the employees affected;
- clear understanding by everyone of their responsibilities.'

So what does this mean for you both as an employee of the organization and as a manager? It means that you have a responsibility for your own self-development, as we noted in Chapter 2, and also for the training and development of the people you manage. This involves identifying, defining and assessing the competences of individuals, including yourself; providing ways for people and yourself to learn and develop skills; and reviewing your own and your staff's development needs and career aspirations. It also involves establishing, defining and reviewing objectives and performance measures, looking at the advantages and disadvantages of existing development provision and investigating new approaches.

In most large UK organizations the idea of the self-managed career has taken root. But it seems from a study that employees still require the appropriate information and advice if they are to manage their own career effectively and use a diverse range of useful sources of guidance.

In order to assess the competence of your staff and set objectives for improvement through training and development, you need to set up some kind of staff appraisal system, as discussed earlier in the chapter. This should also include carrying out a training needs analysis (TNA) in conjunction with the member of staff. Appraisal does not only involve assessment and objective-setting; it involves you in giving your staff constructive feedback on their performance and helping them to increase their potential. It is a contract between you and the individual.

For many managers, embarking on a programme of staff development for the people in their area of responsibility alerts them to their own needs for training and development. As a manager, you are accountable for the performance of your staff; your success depends on their ability. Better trained staff should increase efficiency and even productivity by reducing fatigue and wastage.

The starting point is to identify training and development needs for individual members of staff. Each individual for whom you are responsible is likely to fall into one of three categories in relation to their competence to perform the job. These are:

- Competent to perform current job.
- Not yet competent to perform current job.
- Better than competent at performing current job.

For each category you can provide development as shown in Figure 8.1.

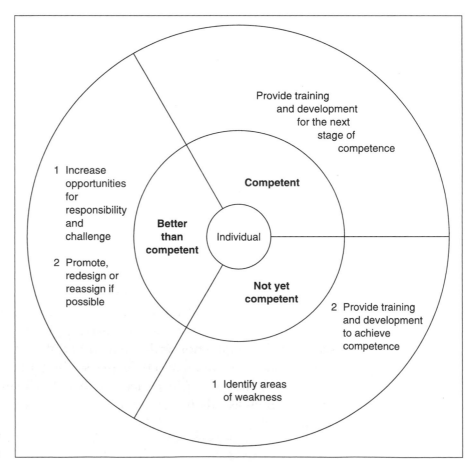

Figure 8.1
Training needs of
individuals

You have to enable your staff to 'grow' in the organization. Somebody who is better than competent in their present job will soon become frustrated and will leave, reduce their performance or become a source of conflict through their personal dissatisfaction. You need to provide recognition of their value and help them to achieve higher objectives. It is not always possible to promote people but you can increase their job satisfaction through delegation or redesigning their jobs (see Chapters 2 and 5).

For those who are not yet competent – and note that we did not use the word 'incompetent' since this implies that they are unlikely to improve – you have to provide opportunities for the individual to develop in the areas of weakness. Most managers find this relatively easy and satisfying unless there is truly no hope of improvement.

The third category – those who are performing their jobs competently – are too often ignored. Even employees can be reluctant to go beyond what is acceptable – doing 'a fair day's work for a fair day's pay'. Unless they can see rewards for achievement which they value, there is no incentive to improve performance. Managers, too, can be reluctant to expend time and energy on people who are performing up to standard. Moving beyond current competence involves both the employee and the manager agreeing on a development plan which the former sees as being in his or her best interests.

In a bid to cut staff turnover on the forecourt, BP has been boosting the career aspirations of its petrol station attendants with a four-star training programme.

Scottish and Newcastle Retail, the pub chain, have introduced a pay-according-to-competence policy and made national vocational qualifications (NVQs) available to all its 25,000 full and part-time staff in an aim to attract good people and cut down turnover. Staff are offered NVQs, for example, which enable them to train in a range of skills such as food-serving, cooking and housekeeping.

METHODS OF DEVELOPMENT

The following are some simple and inexpensive ways in which you can provide training and development for your staff within the organization.

Mentoring

Mentoring is a form of training and development which has been popular in Japan for some time. A mentor is someone, usually a work colleague at the same or a higher level than the individual, for whom he or she is responsible, to whom the individual can go to discuss work-related issues. There is a sense in which the mentoring relationship is similar to that of the 'master–pupil' relationship in medieval times; the pupil is learning from the mentor's experience and the mentor's role is to encourage and nurture his or her protege. Mentors can pass on practical insight derived from experience and can pick up on new ideas and attitudes. They can help their proteges to set themselves realistic expectations and steer them in the right direction as far as their career aspirations are concerned. It can, and should, be a mutually rewarding experience. Many people value being able to pass on what they know, particularly when this is appreciated and others benefit from their knowledge and experience.

An individual may have more than one informal mentor, different people to whom he or she can go for advice and help. This tends to be a proactive approach on the part of the individual who deliberately seeks out others from whom to learn. It may be a formal mentoring arrangement whereby mentors are assigned to new staff as they are recruited. Both forms of mentoring have their benefits and disadvantages. A mentor chosen by his or her protege will have the advantage over one who is 'imposed'. On the other hand, not everyone is proactive in seeking a mentor and a formalized system at least ensures everyone has someone to whom they can go.

It is unfortunate that, although many organizations encourage informal and formal mentoring, few provide training for mentors, make time available in which to undertake this responsibility or give rewards. An untrained mentor can have disastrous effects on new staff and can actually reinforce bad practice rather than encouraging good performance. Mentoring meetings need to be arranged beforehand, programmed into the diary and have a clear agenda relating to the protege's needs. Rewards for mentoring are often intrinsic, in that mentors value the increased responsibility, whereas in Japan some companies reward the mentor when the protege achieves promotion.

Job or work rotation

This involves staff trying out a number of different jobs or different parts of the same job to get an understanding of other kinds of task and of how they all fit together. In either case, someone will have to be responsible for training the person in the new job or work.

Secondment

This is a more formal type of job rotation in which a member of staff is seconded to another job on a short- or long-term basis, perhaps while someone is ill or when a member of staff has left.

Special assignments or projects

These can involve the person in different work which may suit that person's particular skills.

'Sitting by Nellie'

This form of training, which is similar to mentoring, exists in many organizations, notably those involved with production or manufacturing. The trainee is assigned to an experienced member of staff who should be given training in how to train and time in which to do it (but often is not).

Coaching

To be effective, this form of training needs to be planned and time should be allowed for the coach to develop staff. It involves consciously seeking out opportunities for developing people, training the person to do the job and giving him or her impartial feedback on performance. It has the advantage of developing the coach as well as the trainee.

There are many other forms of training and staff development demonstrations, discussion groups, presentations, simulations, assessment centres, computer-aided training, action learning groups, in-tray exercises – but they all need to be seen in an overall training and development context. Part of your job as a manager is not only to identify training needs but to plan and implement a cost-effective and ongoing training programme, using resources both inside the organization and outside it as well.

The difficulties of training fire service officers to take charge in a major incident are being overcome by virtual reality. A virtual reality training programme, developed by the Fire Service College and Colt VR, uses desktop-based scenarios to test officers' crisis-management skills.

Financial services company, Beneficial Bank, has used a charity event run with Wiltshire Police to improve team working and establish better communication between bank managers. The one-day event involved a competition between 30 managers from the company's western district and Wiltshire Constabulary's air support unit. Participants took part in driving, fitness and shooting contests and money was raised for two local charities. 'The challenge provided Beneficial with an ideal team-building opportunity for colleagues who would only normally meet in a working environment', said Reading branch manager.

STAFF DEVELOPMENT OUTSIDE THE ORGANIZATION

Many organizations use a combination of in-house specialized training and external training providers: the balance is up to you, the organization, its needs, the needs of the individual and the training budget.

The range of external providers is immense, including local colleges and universities, business schools, commercial training organizations, professional institutions and employers' federations. Your first contact when looking for external training provision should be your local Learning and Skills Council (LSC), which have replaced the Training and Enterprise Councils which carried out this role in the 1990s. They act as 'brokers' between organizations that have identified training needs and training providers on a local and national basis.

Some organizations, such as those involved in the hotel and catering industry, clothing, construction and road transport have their own Industry Training Boards (ITBs) which encourage industry-related training by line managers. There are also a number of voluntary training arrangements, such as the Local Government Training Board and the Dairy Trade Federation.

The LSCs will encourage employers to become Investors in People. 'Investors in People' (IiP) was launched in October 1991 in an attempt to persuade employers to take an interest in training and developing their employees. In order to qualify as Investors in People, organizations have to make a public commitment from the top to develop all employees to achieve their business objectives; they have regularly to review the training and development needs of all employees and take action to train and develop staff on recruitment and throughout their employment; they also have to evaluate their investment in training and development to assess achievement and improve future effectiveness.

For some organizations, the good practice encouraged by IiP was already part of their policy; companies such as Distillers and Vintners of Essex and Nissan Motor Manufacturing (UK) claimed that they needed to make only a few alterations to current practice in order to comply with IiP standards. Many others have failed to meet the very high standards demanded by the initiative.

One of the most important training developments in the 1990s was the emergence of National Vocational Qualifications (NVQs or SVQs in Scotland), actively promoted and supported by the government. These have been developed in response to the confusing array of qualifications supposedly related to organizational needs. Vocational qualifications are directly related to the needs of the employer.

The retail chain W. H. Smith offers an NVQ award for its 13,000 shop assistants which it runs in addition to its own training programme.

Competence-based materials, compatible with the NVQ system, have been produced for use on the Association of Accounting Technician's examination syllabus.

The National Retail Training Council and City and Guilds have developed NVQ Certificates for supervisors and managers in the retail trade. The competence-based qualification has no pre-entry requirements, age or time restrictions, takes into account previous experience and allows candidates to work at their own pace.

A competence-based NVQ Certificate is now available by distance-learning for managers in the National Health Service.

Investigate

Find out what training opportunities exist locally which might be of use to you in developing yourself and your staff.

Not all external training needs to involve people being away from work: indeed, with the advent of NVQs, it is preferable that individuals remain at work while they are undergoing training. One effect of the introduction of NVQs/SVQs has been the development of managers as assessors for these qualifications. Instead of sending staff off to the local college or buying in training from outside, organizations can train their own staff and assess them in the workplace. There are also a wide range of distance and open learning training packages available, many of which only involve people in off-site training outside normal working hours.

Help available

Apart from LSCs and Industrial Training Boards or industry-specific training organizations, the following organizations can provide information and support on training matters:

- The Chartered Institute of Personnel and Development
- The Industrial Society
- The British Association for Commercial and Industrial Education
- The Institute of Employment Studies

Local libraries are also a useful source of information on provision of training and development near your place of work.

Summary

Performance management is seen as a means of bringing together the various personnel interventions that go to make up a human relations policy, and integrate them in a way which maximizes overall performance. However, this is not an easy task, and may not be successful, especially if imposed from the top without any sense of ownership further down the organization. In addition, measuring performance has its own problems. Nevertheless, some framework for evaluating performance is necessary.

Appraisal systems should be designed to focus employees on both their short- and long-term objectives and career goals. Well-designed appraisal systems benefit the organization, managers and individuals in different ways and need to fulfil certain key objectives if they are to be successful. Appraisal is concerned with setting objectives for individuals for an agreed period and monitoring progress towards these objectives on a regular basis in an atmosphere of trust and cooperation between the appraiser and the individual.

This trust and cooperation also involves being able to provide staff with constructive feedback on their performance, whether it be good or bad. This feedback will only be effective if performance itself can be measured in ways which are truly objective and which can identify above- and below-average competence in individuals.

A rewards system should be seen as doing more than merely paying workers, but needs to take account of their need for intrinsic as well as other extrinsic rewards. These are, however, likely to vary between individuals, and moreover, rewards systems need regular reviewing if they are not to lose their effectiveness. Moreover, the rewards system needs to reflect a range of organizational objectives.

Continuous self- and staff-development are essential to continuous performance improvement. Present government initiatives have recognized this fact and provided encouragement for training and development, unfortunately not supported by financial incentives for organizations.

Your own self-development needs to be related to your personal strengths and weaknesses and to your individual career aspirations. This requires planning your career progression, either within your present organization or outside it, and setting your career goals.

Programmes of training and development for staff need to be related to individual training needs and aspirations. Induction training and mentoring are two methods of providing training for new staff, although mentoring arrangements often continue beyond the initial training period.

There is a wide range of training and development opportunities which can be provided by the organization or by other providers. This external training can be industry- or sector-specific, or it may be more general in focus. There are also opportunities for managers to devise competence-based programmes leading to the award of an NVQ/SVQ and for them to be trained as assessors in this form of staff development.

Activities

1 Draw up a list of the different ways in which your organization measures people's performance.
2 Either suggest improvements to an existing appraisal system in your own organization, or design an appraisal system which would meet the objectives outlined in this chapter.
3 Identify the objectives which your organization reflects in its rewards system.
4 Identify the training needs for individuals within your area of responsibility.
5 Draw up a list of training provisions which would meet the needs of staff you identified in (4) above, using internal and external training resources where appropriate.

CHAPTER 9

Managing challenging situations

INTRODUCTION

This chapter moves away from the assumption that the world of work is reasonably stable and that the role of the manager is to lead in the definition and achievement of objectives through people. This chapter introduces some potentially problematic issues for managers in which their assumptions of predictability and control may need to be modified and they may need to respond to situations rather than creating them. There are three main clusters of problem areas: one dealing with diversity within the workforce; one dealing with the dynamics of organizational life such as power, conflict and stress; and the third dealing with the institutionalization of issues such as grievances and discipline.

In the present chapter, we deal with the following issues:

- Managing diversity.
- Managing multicultural teams.
- Cultural distinctions.
- Equal opportunities.
- Managing power.
- Managing stress.
- Managing conflict.
- Dealing with unions.
- Handling grievances.

■ Handling discipline.

■ Dismissal.

MANAGING DIVERSITY

Many of the issues which we have dealt with in the preceding chapters take on an additional dimension when the workgroup with which you are involved is diverse in its make-up. In the 'old' days, groups in a factory or office or mine used to be homogeneous and very often from the same locality, who knew each other from their background. This is now much less true, and certainly cannot be taken for granted; managers cannot assume that all the people who work for them can be treated as a homogenous group. The workforces of all organizations are growing more diverse. Patterns of migration, changing legal norms and the internationalization of industries have stimulated the movement of human resources across organizational borders and across national boundaries. There are many different aspects of diversity, encompassing gender, ethnic origin, age, language, physical ability, and sexual orientation. Different shift patterns, different job functions, different grades of work can also constitute differences that require the management of diversity. Perhaps even more specifically, different people have different personalities, which may need different management styles to get the best out of them. Managing diversity:

■ aims to ensure that all staff maximize their potential and contribute to the organization;

■ concentrates on movement within the organization, its culture and the meeting of business objectives;

■ concerns all staff, particularly managers;

■ does not rely on positive action or affirmative action and provides a vision.

Legislation and the high profile of equal opportunities in the UK has had both positive and negative effects on the way people view each other. On the one hand, there is now widespread recognition that discrimination at work on the grounds of gender, race or ability alone is unjust, although the practice still continues. Paradoxically, however, the grouping of minorities such as 'women' or 'ethnic' or 'disabled' has produced stereotypical responses. For example, there has been a considerable increase in courses for women returning to work after a career break; but not all women require courses, nor are they all likely to need courses on the same topics. More recent thinking has moved towards 'managing diversity' – recognizing and valuing differences in people and their unique contributions to the workforce.

However, differences, particularly if not well-managed or recognized can also create discrimination or conflict which may develop into grievances or require taking some form of disciplinary action and possibly lead to legal consequences. We deal with this eventuality in the next chapter. Too often, people concentrate on the negative aspects of differences, such as not understanding the language another person speaks, or their religious practices or their lifestyle, without seeing the positive aspects of having access to different viewpoints and perspectives. Unfortunately, at the heart of many organizational conflicts are differences concerning values, beliefs and interests.

Differences have disadvantages, but they can also have considerable advantages. In particular, they can reflect the real world much more fully than a homogeneous group that can easily lose sight of wider issues. They are also likely to be less inward looking and produce a wider range of perspectives. Unless there is recognition of these issues, corporate structure become 'climbing-frames for politicians' and a danger that cloning of those already in power eliminates diversity.

Kandola and Fullerton (1994) have noted a range of successful initiatives for organizations pursuing diversity policies:

- Training trainers in equal opportunities.
- Introducing equal rights and benefits for part-time workers as compared to full-timers.
- Allowing flexibility in dress or uniform requirements.
- Allowing time off for caring for dependants beyond those required by law.
- Benefits provided for employees' partners are equally available to same-sex and different-sex partners.
- Providing specialized equipment for those with disabilities.
- Employing helpers for those that need them.
- Providing assistance with child care.
- Allowing staff to take career breaks.
- Eliminating age discrimination from selection decisions.

Nevertheless, Kandola and Fullerton also argue that an organization that manages diversity effectively should adopt a 'no preferential treatment' view that does not give individuals preference only because they are members of a minority group. For example, assertiveness training is very often provided only, or mainly, for women. If assertiveness is a valued organizational characteristic, training should be provided for anyone who needs it.

Investigate

Think about people in your own area of responsibility. Which of them would you describe as 'different' from yourself in terms of gender, race or ability? What characteristics do you value in them?

MANAGING MULTICULTURAL TEAMS

If you work all, or most of the time with the same team of colleagues, you know each other's strengths and weaknesses. If you are part of a new team, brought together as part of a project, you will need time to get to know one another. A third – and increasing – possibility is working in a multicultural team with people of different nationalities, which brings its own challenges. Working in a multicultural team increases the number of different assumptions and expectations about working practices.

It is quite common in the UK for managers to work on after 'office' hours; in fact, it is often seen as a sign of dedication and commitment. Scandinavian managers, on the other hand, are used to finishing work at somewhere between 4.30 p.m. and 5 p.m. and consider people who stay on beyond that time as inefficient or incompetent.

In the USA and the UK, team members usually refer to each other by their first names. This is not the case in Germany and some Scandinavians expect to be called by their last name only. Even assumptions about leadership and authority can differ quite widely amongst European member states. Team leaders in the Netherlands, Scandinavia and the UK adopt a more participative and consultative style of leadership than their counterparts in Germany. Dutch managers are usually fairly relaxed about who is, or who should be, in charge; Germans, however, operate within a much more formal hierarchical structure and the French do not expect their decisions to be questioned when they are in a position of authority.

A further complexity with multicultural teams is created by language. While English is considered to be the 'lingua franca' in the business world, not everyone can be expected to speak or understand it to the same extent. This convention of conducting business in

English has made English-speakers lazy about acquiring skills in languages other than their own. There is a considerable danger that not everyone in a multicultural team shares the same understanding about problems and decisions or that some people, for whom English is a second language, cannot express themselves adequately. Forming a multicultural team is likely to take more time and a greater degree of sensitivity from the participants than you would expect when creating a team with shared cultural experience.

The Personnel Manager of Rover Group's English–Bulgarian joint venture, based in Daru Car, sees some of the most important lessons learned from the experience as:

- the benefits of sending Bulgarian team leaders to England to encourage motivation and team working;
- the problems of making Bulgarian team leaders more concerned for their team members – in a society with high inflation, low confidence and a struggling economy, the tendency is to grab whatever you can and still ask for more while it is still there;
- the need to temper a 'we do it in England, therefore it is best' approach with Bulgaria's cultural background and behaviour.

Working abroad, or working in your own country with managers from other countries, creates culture shock because your expectations of the right way of doing things differs from those of other countries. Those difficulties are, of course, exacerbated by language. The old joke about the United States and England being countries separated by a common language has the major merit of reminding us that it is all too easy to believe that another person has understood you. When the other person's language is not English, the difficulties that arise are often clearer, although equally the subject of horror stories or jokes (Mumford, 1997).

If you are recruiting staff abroad, there are a number of factors of which you need to be aware. These include:

- knowledge about local labour markets in the country in which you are recruiting;
- knowledge of local education systems and the status of educational qualifications;
- the need to consider language and cultural differences in an interview situation;

■ avoiding the use of recruitment methods which are accepted in the UK but are counter to other cultures.

CULTURAL DISTINCTIONS

Diversity sees a workforce as composed of heterogeneous individuals from different backgrounds, whereas cultural differences assume that groups are reasonably homogeneous but differ between themselves. The easiest way to think in terms of cultural differences is on the basis of nationality, but given the polyglot nature of many countries, cultural differences also apply within countries. Geert Hofstede (1980) a Dutch social psychologist, conducted a study of IBM employees in 70 countries with the intention of measuring cultural differences. The use of IBM was to avoid any impact of company culture, and to make matters even more common, only the sales and service employees were involved. He identified four basic dimensions of the differences between national cultures.

■ Power distance, is concerned with how far the culture encourages superiors to exert power. In a country where power distance is large, being a boss is about exerting power, but in a small power distance country, superiors and subordinates consider each other to be colleagues, so that the inequality between them is minimized and superiors are accessible.

■ Uncertainty avoidance raises the issue of the extent to which a culture encourages change and risk-taking. In strong uncertainty avoidance countries people feel threatened by uncertain situations and experience high levels of stress in change, whereas in a weak uncertainty avoidance culture the uncertainty which is inherent in life is easily accepted, which means less stress and less need for rules.

■ The individualism–collectivism dimension is the extent to which a culture encourages individual as opposed to collective concerns. In an individualistic culture identity is based on the individual, whereas a collectivist culture is characterized by a tighter social framework and the emphasis is on belonging to the group and being a good member of it.

■ Masculinity–femininity is somewhat unfortunately named since it follows the stereotyping of gender roles. Masculinity has an emphasis on the achievement of goals and a focus on winning as opposed to losing. Success, money, and material standards are important. Femininity shows more concern for the whole process and context and looks for ways of satisfying everyone. Here the quality of life matters more than money, and people and the environment are also important.

Out of these four categorizations, Hofstede suggested four distinctive models:

- A group of countries centred in Asia, where there is high power distance, low individualism, medium masculinity and low uncertainty avoidance, and where the organizational model is like a family and the key is the leader or father figure.
- A Germanic group characterized by low power distance, medium individualism, high masculinity and high uncertainty avoidance, in which there is a desire to seek rules and procedures which avoid the personal exercise of power and operate rather like a machine.
- In the Latin and Near Eastern group typified by high power distance, low individualism, medium masculinity and high uncertainty avoidance, power relationships and work processes are defined and the result is similar to a human pyramid.
- Finally in the Anglo group of countries, low power distance, high individualism, high masculinity and low uncertainty avoidance leads to a market analogy with continuous bargaining between members.

Obviously Hofstede's work over-simplifies the actual situation in countries, since there is a range within any country, and also creates a risk of stereotyping, but the categories are nevertheless useful for managers to help them to understand some of the causes of differences. The implications of Hofstede's research are that cultural differences do have a significant impact on how organizations operate, and also therefore on policies for managing people. For an excellent review of the implications of Hofstede's cultural categories for HR policies, see Schuler (2001), especially Table 16.3.

EQUAL OPPORTUNITIES AS THE BASIS FOR MANAGING DIVERSITY

Equal opportunities are at the heart of a policy for dealing with the management of diversity or cultural differences, and many organizations have policies covering the area to assert their intention to provide equal opportunities for all categories of staff. The term is sometimes held to concentrate on avoiding discrimination or unfairness as between groups, but it should be more proactive than this. It should involve acknowledging, tolerating and indeed welcoming differences. It can also involve being proactive, as in what the Americans call 'affirmative action', such as boosting the proportion of minority groups in employment. It also needs to emphasize that equal opportunities is not just something to be pursued by management, but is the responsibility of all workers towards each other. Bullying and harassment are practices which are sometimes pursued by managers, but much more frequently by workers or groups of workers against each other.

Investigate

Does your organization have an equal opportunities policy? If so, which groups does it cover and on what personnel issues? Does it have any means of monitoring equal opportunities? Who has responsibility for doing this?

As well as enjoining against discrimination, policy in this area also needs to define best practice. Thus the Equal Opportunities Commission and the Commission for Racial Equality have set out some basic principles for selection interviewing, summarized below:

- The same kinds of questions should be asked across all racial groups and to both men and women.
- Questions should all be relevant to the job description and employee specification.
- Interviewers should avoid questions related to their perceptions of different cultures, although they need to be aware of religious and cultural differences in candidates.
- Questions should not be based on assumptions about traditional women's roles in the home and family.

Similarly, the Employers' Forum on Disability have produced guidance on disability etiquette in interviewing. This includes:

- Conducting interviews with disabled people as you would with anyone else.
- Emphasizing abilities, achievements and individual qualities but avoiding putting people with disabilities on a pedestal.
- Remembering that questions concerning a candidate's disability should be restricted to those relevant to the job.
- Not making assumptions about a candidate's ability to perform certain tasks.
- Not relying on intermediaries for information or opinions about a disabled candidate's capacity to perform the job; using your own judgement from discussion with the candidate.
- Not requiring application forms, letters etc. to be handwritten unless this is essential to performance of the job.

We now move to the second cluster of problematic issues in managing people, namely dealing with the management of power, stress, and conflict.

MANAGING POWER

Power is a necessity in organizations if objectives are to be achieved because it gives a focus to the social system that exists in the organization or the unit within it. Managers need power to do their jobs effectively, and they need to know what creates power and how to use it. Power is the capacity to affect other people's behaviour without their consent, and is a personal attribute which has an effect on others. But managers need not be the only focus of power in units; individuals or groups may be able to exercise power formally or informally. So what are the sources of power in an organization?

Authority is defined in terms of the hierarchy and structure of the organization and is dependent on its resources. It gives the right to control finance, people, information etc., but it is only legitimated if others recognize and concede it. Authority is therefore limited, and does not guarantee power, although it is obviously an important source of power.

- Physical characteristics, including intelligence and physical presence.

- Personality, which involves both emotional dimensions and behaviour, and can provide charisma, which is a high level of ability to influence people though personality.
- Achievements and reputation.
- Rewards, such as the capacity to reward people financially or psychologically.

The obverse of this, the power to punish or criticize, can also be an important source of power.

- Access to important people elsewhere, but usually higher up in the organization, or outside of it.
- Access to resources, especially information.
- Interpersonal, political, and social skills.
- Wealth.
- Expertise, based on knowledge, skill or experience.

Managers spend a considerable amount of time and effort in trying to expand their power and increase its legitimation. People are on the whole happy if a manager's power is used in their interests and that of the organization. But power games in organizations can be damaging to its effectiveness. Moreover others, either individuals or groups, in your area of responsibility may also have some of the attributes of power noted above, so there may be alternative locations for the exercise of power. Indeed, it is likely that there are several alternative sources of power in the different interest groups in the unit, and conflict may be the outcome, as noted below. Moreover, because power depends to a considerable extent on the legitimation of others, this can be withdrawn if the manager does something which is unacceptable to the group and his power will have been diminished. Perhaps equally importantly, their respect for him may have been diminished, and respect is a key dimension of legitimation. Managers therefore need to be aware of the limits of their legitimated power. They need to use political skills and other sources of power as well as authority to influence behaviour. Authority alone is unlikely to be a source of effective power for very long.

Power games are however likely to be part of organizational life, and managers must be aware of their implications if they are to be effective. Baddely and James (1987) suggested two types of action in organizations, those where people are acting with integrity and in the organization's interests, and those where they are 'playing games' and seeking to advance their own interests at the expense of others. There are also those who are politically aware and those who are politically naïve. Baddely and James suggest animal analogies for the four types thus created. Thus those who are playing games but are politically aware are called foxes, while those who are playing games but are politically naïve are donkeys. Those who are acting with integrity but who are politically naïve are sheep, while those who are both acting with integrity and are politically aware are called an owl. Clearly managers need to have some idea as to who is what in this classification, and indeed to be aware of how their own actions will be viewed.

Investigate   What are the sources of power in your unit? How concentrated is it? How can you respond to it?

MANAGING STRESS

Stress is a feature of organizational life; most managers are likely to find themselves facing stress as an issue in their organization; if they do not they are either very good managers, or exceptionally lucky. Moreover the implications of stress can be very significant personally, organizationally, legally and financially.

The Times of 5 December 2000 reported that:
'A teacher who was forced to retire early after two breakdowns has been awarded . . . £254,362 for the intolerable working conditions at the 'school'. Her union said they were dealing at any one time with 120 stress-related compenzation claims.

In 1996, 60 per cent of people in employment suffered from work-related stress according to a report from the union MSF. Seventy-one per cent of respondents said stress levels in their workplace were higher than five years ago and nearly two-thirds said they were higher than in 1994.

A survey of 4,600 Barclays Bank managers revealed that a quarter have received medical treatment for stress-related illnesses in the past five years. Nearly half the managers felt insecure in their jobs and 19 per cent worked up to, and sometimes over, 25 hours a week overtime. Barclays has contracted a counselling service to cope with employees' problems.

More generally, it is estimated that stress-related illness costs Britain about £7 billion a year, of which some £4 billion is estimated to come from the 180 million working days lost annually as a result of stress at work, about half of the total number of days lost. Moreover, this figure has been rising, in spite of higher living standards and more highly regulated working conditions. And it is not only direct losses of days: about 40 per cent of staff turnover is said to be due to stress, and many of the inefficiencies of people's daily activities can also be associated with stress. Frequently work is not the only factor, and sources of stress can be brought into work by domestic or community issues. But work is still arguably the key source and is often associated with interpersonal aspects of the work situation.

So what is stress? The Health and Safety Executive defines stress as 'The reaction people have to excessive pressures or other types of demand placed on them. It arises when they worry they can't cope'. But having too little to do or lack of any variety in one's work can also cause stress, by creating boredom and dissatisfaction. Some pressure is necessary for optimum performance, and it is obviously difficult to get the balance right. How people cope with stress depends on their personality, their ability to accept change and their tolerance of ambiguity. Some people thrive in stressful situations, as is often said of high achievers and of top sportsmen or women, while others cannot cope.

Research by the industrial psychologist, Peter Warr (1987), has identified nine features of jobs which influence stress. These are:

- Low job discretion, i.e. little freedom to make decisions or to exercise control over work.
- Low use of skills.
- Low or high work demands.
- Low task variety, i.e. repetitive, monotonous work.
- High uncertainty about how well or poorly you are performing and about the survival of the company and your place in it.
- Low pay, creating difficult financial circumstances.
- Poor working conditions, especially noisy, hot, wet or dangerous environments.
- Low interpersonal support at work.
- Carrying out a job which is perceived as being of low value in society.

In isolation, any one of these features is unlikely to cause severe stress. Rather, it is the combination of factors which lead to this condition. In particular, Warr found that high work demands combined with low job discretion was particularly stressful. To this list above might be added the long hours culture of much of British industry by which British workers spend more hours per day at work than their Continental counterparts, with one in six working more than 48 hours a week.

Investigate

Do any of these conditions apply in your unit? What might be done about them? How might you respond if they cannot be changed?

A Chartered Institute of Personnel and Development survey suggests that workaholics are jeopardizing their careers and their home lives. Nearly a quarter of self-confessed workaholics do not take a single paid day's holiday a year.

British Telecom won the 2001 Employer of the Year Award largely as a result of family-friendly policies including a Work-Life Balance initiative.

The first step in coping with stress is to recognize that it exists in yourself or in others. Stress is now accepted as a physiological response which can become an illness. Some of the wide range of the body's reactions to stress are:

- Difficulty sleeping.
- Voice tremor.
- Over-sensitivity.
- Low self-control.
- Increased heart and blood pressure.
- Difficulty concentrating.
- Increased sweat.
- Use of alcohol for relaxation.
- Feeling tired, overworked or bored.
- Increased irritability.
- Increased dependency on cigarettes, alcohol or tranquillizers.
- Anxiety.
- Depression.
- Swings of mood.
- Poor appetite or excessive eating.
- Headaches.
- Stomach problems.

Investigate
Are any of your staff or indeed you yourself suffering from any of these symptoms? If they or you are suffering from a number of them, it may be time to recommend or seek medical advice.

Some aspects of stress can be minimized through improved job design (see Chapter 5) whereas others require medical help. Work-related stress is an illness and should be treated as such; it is not a weakness. The longer it is allowed to go untreated, the longer it may take for the individual to recover so you are not doing yourself or your organization any favours by ignoring the symptoms.

How to manage stress is largely about avoiding it rather than dealing with its consequences. The most important factor in avoiding stress lies in the nature of the organization itself in providing an open, dynamic environment with a clear sense of direction. But there are also a number of specific ways that can be introduced by the individual manager:

- Providing a people-oriented leadership.
- Putting people in jobs which are within their capabilities.
- Re-evaluating people's motivation and not placing too many demands on them.
- Redesigning jobs to make them more acceptable; in particular by removing ambiguities or conflict in the role or by increasing the amount of autonomy that workers have.
- Counselling people to enable them to talk about their problems, either with a mentor, or with a member of the personnel department. Medical attention may be necessary in some circumstances.
- Giving workers better training to enable them to do the job better; this may also go for managers, for whom training may enable them to see the needs of their staff.
- Appraisal or other performance reviews which allow a dialogue between the manager and the worker about their performance and any problems with it.
- Examining the work–life balance of employees.

Ideally, the intention is to build up in people a resilience based on self-awareness and self-esteem which breeds a positive outlook towards life and which in turn which enables them to tolerate more stress. At the same time, of course, the organization needs to work to reduce the causes of stress.

MANAGING CONFLICT

Conflict is generally accepted as an inevitable part of organizational life, and the term brings with it connotations of antagonism and undesirability. However, it should not automatically be thought that all conflict is dysfunctional. Constructive conflict can introduce new solutions to a problem, define power relationships within a group, bring non-rational emotional dimensions into the open, and provide for the release of catharsis by identifying long-established conflict. On the other hand destructive conflict can result in a loss of the main objectives in the pursuit of sub-group interests, induce people to be defensive, and eventually result in the disintegration of the group.

Sources of conflict in organizations

These are endemic in organizations and while some can be superficial, many go very deep into our personal identity

Interpersonal differences

For all kinds of reasons, some people don't get on with others – you can't expect to like everyone you meet or work with, nor to be liked by everyone else. There are differences in personality, temperament, outlook and beliefs which make this impossible. Recognizing these differences is half the battle and, as a manager, trying not to force people with real interpersonal differences which cannot be resolved to work together.

Misunderstandings

These can arise because of different languages or accents or simply because people genuinely didn't understand what was said or implied. Often, misunderstandings can be cleared up if a third party realizes what has happened and can persuade the protagonists that it was, simply, 'a misunderstanding'.

Differences in values and beliefs

Values and beliefs are shaped by experience and upbringing and, thus, are likely to differ considerably. In a study of managers on courses run by the Swedish company, SAS, participants were asked to list the values most important to them. Most of the Swedish managers chose honesty as the most important whereas North American managers chose competition, liberty and freedom and did not mention honesty in the top fifteen. Competition was not an important value for the Swedish managers (Mumford, 1997). Values and beliefs are usually deeply rooted and difficult to change; again they need to be recognized and respected if conflict is to be avoided. Experiments have shown that when people are allocated to a group, they discriminate, perhaps initially unconsciously, in favour of it and against other groups. Just consider how the inhabitants of one nation think of themselves in relation to other nations, and obtain personal self-esteem by identifying with their own country. It is the same at work; even if people are allocated on a random basis, being a member of a group gives them identity and self-esteem and makes them feel different to other groups.

Differences in interest

When a conflict arises, it is common to find that people have different interests in its resolution − or in its continuation. Interests may be personal or departmental, but they are likely to centre on competition of an economic nature. When these economic differences are added to the psychological differences noted above, there is latent conflict in many situations in the workplace. The most basic competition is for scarce resources, which may be financial, such as pay, or non-financial such as additional staff. Each group will have its own goals, and the extent to which another group interferes with the achievement of the group goals will be an indication of the extent of competition. As well as economic conflict, there may be conflict over objectives, especially if two groups need to co-operate to achieve some wider goal. Thus the efficiency of one group in using a machine may be dependent on receiving constant supplies from another group, but it may not be efficient for the second group to make the supplies constantly available. Thus the two groups have potentially incompatible objectives. You are likely to have some elements of such interdependence between groups or individuals in your area of responsibility.

Investigate

Think about a conflict at work. Which of the above sources do you think was at the root of the conflict?

These differences between groups or individuals have effects which are perceptual, emotional, and behavioural. The perceptions created by group identification will be exacerbated by group competition. At the emotional level, emotions relation to the other group are likely to be negative, creating an 'us' against 'them' situation. This in turn leads to behavioural outcomes which may be of various kinds. Much depends on whether the group is seen by itself to be 'winning' or 'losing' Sometimes both sides feel that they are losing. The 'winners' feel satisfied, with a release of the tension built up during competition, and group cohesion may be increased. The 'losers' may wish to deny the outcome, or look for someone to blame, either internally or possibly outside the group, e.g. the manager acting as referee, and tension is likely to remain, while there will be a desire for regrouping and a chance to overturn the result. For both groups, inter-group rivalry is likely to increase.

In a survey in 2001, 1 in 10 of British workers claimed to have been bullied at work in the previous six months.

So what does the manager do in these circumstances, which are likely to be fairly frequent and in some cases on-going? None of the answers are without their own problems.

Try to ensure that both sides of a conflict gain by co-operation rather than having a competition where one side wins and the other loses. This may not be easy because of the psychological factors, but it will at least reduce the tension.

■ Provide open communication between and with the groups, if necessary with the manager acting as a mediator to identify the issues and clarify the organizational objectives. Again, this may be easier said than done, but it should at least be tried.
■ Use power to resolve conflict. This may have the advantage of being relatively quick, but it also carries the potential for resentment and an on-going unsatisfactory situation.
■ Build trust. This is the most desirable way to resolve the problems, but as the longevity of ethnic, religious and class

feuds around the world reminds us, it is often very difficult to achieve. Trust takes a long time to establish, and requires open communication as a pre-requisite.

■ Problem solving through negotiation. Most situations are not in fact zero sum, i.e. where if one side gains, the other side loses an equal amount. Most situations can be turned with careful thought to one where both sides can gain something, even if one gains more than the other. This will also probably involve compromise, a key dimension of successful negotiation.

We now move to the third cluster of problem areas, that of providing structures and procedures to deal with disagreements at work. Having sensible institutions and procedures which are understood and trusted by all concerned is arguably the best safeguard against the escalation of a minor incident into a serious problem.

DEALING WITH UNIONS

There is still a residual view that unions are anti-capitalist and anti-managerial, striving to overturn the existing economic system. This has never been true other than in a miniscule percentage of union membership, but it is even less true now. Over the last 20 years, British unions have lost power and membership but have also become much concerned with two broad objectives: working with management collectively to improve standards and efficiency, and helping their members as individuals through a range of advisory services. A recent survey carried out for the TUC found that people did not want an adversarial relationship with their employer. More than 70 per cent of both members and non-members preferred the statement 'We work with management to improve the workplace and working conditions' to an alternative 'We defend workers against unfair treatment by management'. A good company recognizes that it needs to hear the voice of its workforce and in many cases a union is best placed to provide this. Nevertheless, the decline of unions in the last 20 years has also seen a rise in the interaction with workers as individuals rather than as members of groups, and a growing use of the term 'employee relations' to replace the older collective term of 'industrial relations'.

Industrial relations can be seen as a system of institutions, rules, and procedures, and both formal and informal processes, by which the regulation of employment through collective bargaining and conflict resolution takes place. A formal set of written agreements may well be complemented by the climate of relationships between the parties and elements of custom and practice whose origins might be lost in the mists of time. Much of the history of British industry in the last century was determined in considerable part by major issues of industrial relations, such as the extent of managerial control or 'right to manage', the introduction of new working practices, and conflicts over wage levels. We will not go into industrial relations at length, because it is likely to be organized at levels above you, and also because a discussion of its institutions will not be directly applicable to many managers. Instead, we will concentrate on the implications of two dimensions of dealing with your employees with which you are very likely to have to deal, namely the management of grievances and discipline.

Investigate

What is the structure of industrial relations in your organization? If there are no unions, is there any other mechanism through which employees can express themselves collectively?

MANAGING GRIEVANCES

A member of your staff comes to you to complain that his weekly pay packet contains less than he thinks it ought to. You remind him that he took half a day's leave earlier in the week and he goes back to work satisfied with your answer.

A group of staff come to you with the complaint that your suppliers are failing to meet deadlines and work is being held up as a result. You promise to investigate the problem and reassure them that it will not affect their pay until the matter is settled. You discover their grievance is genuine and put pressure on the suppliers to conform to deadlines. Work returns to normal. (Examples from Thomson and Murray, 1976.)

A grievance begins as an expression of dissatisfaction by an individual or group of employees in respect of 'any measure or situation which directly affects or may affect the conditions of employment of one or several workers in the undertaking when that measure or situation appears contrary to the provisions of an applicable collective agreement or of an individual contract of employment, to work rules, to laws or regulations or to the custom or usage of the occupation or country' (International Labour Organization, 1965). A grievance may arise within an industrial relations structure in which there are shop stewards, union branches, and full-time officials. Or it may arise in a context where there is no system of worker representation and individuals are acting on their own. Or there may be some intermediate situation. The potential for grievances exists irrespective of the institutional background.

A grievance usually starts with some kind of trigger in the form of management or peer action which gives rise to individual or group dissatisfaction. If the dissatisfaction is initially experienced by an individual, the person may seek allies to support him or her in their opinions or may go to his or her manager and voice the dissatisfaction. At this stage, it may be no more than a 'dissatisfaction' with some aspect of the individual's working environment which can be handled sensitively and the dissatisfaction reduced or eliminated if it is within the manager's control. If the dissatisfaction is more widespread, the kind of group cohesion described in Chapter 6 can occur and the discontent can grow accordingly. Again, it may be possible for the manager to avert this growing dissatisfaction or it may be necessary to consult with colleagues or people higher up in the organization or turn the matter over to a superior. It all depends on the extent and the level of dissatisfaction and the way in which it is handled as to whether it becomes a more formalized and serious grievance. As a manager, you can often prevent conflict from escalating by becoming aware of it at an early stage and trying to resolve it before it becomes a formal grievance.

The Advisory, Conciliation and Arbitration Service in its Advisory Handbook on Discipline and Grievances at Work (2001) has provided a checklist which employers should consider when handling a grievance:

- Ensure everyone who might deal with a grievance is trained and understands the procedure.
- Set down simple procedures in writing which provide for prompt and confidential handling of grievances.
- Consider whether separate procedures might be necessary for sensitive areas such as discrimination, bullying and harassment, and 'whistle-blowing'. A nominated contact within the organization may be appropriate for fair treatment issues.
- Give every worker a copy of the procedure or make it readily accessible.

- If there is a grievance applying to more than one person consider whether it should be resolved with any recognized trade union(s).
- Deal with grievances informally if possible – a discussion between worker and line manager is often the best way to proceed. If the line manager is the subject of the grievance the organization should have a standby procedure – perhaps referring the matter to another senior manager who can decide who can best deal with the grievance.
- If the matter needs a more formal approach, follow the procedure.
- The worker should put grievances raised under the formal procedure in writing.
- Hold a hearing in private. Make sure the worker is informed of their right to be accompanied.
- Have as open a discussion as possible about how the grievance might be resolved.
- Be calm and fair and do not make snap decisions.
- Ensure the hearing does not turn into any kind of disciplinary procedure.
- Seek external help if necessary.
- In form the worker when he or she can expect a response.
- Respond to the worker's grievance in writing within the time limits specified in the procedure, and tell the worker of any further stages under the procedure.
- Keep simple records, ensuring security, confidentiality and that they conform to the requirements of the Data Protection Act 1998.

All organizations must provide employees with details of how to go about seeking redress of any work-related grievance, apart from those governed separately under the Health and Safety at Work Act 1974, and these grievance procedures should be agreed with representatives of any trade unions concerned. The procedures should be formal and should be given to employees in writing as part of their terms and conditions of service. Since 1993, employers have also been required to ensure that employees' written terms and conditions of employment include the name of 'a person to whom the employee can apply for the purposes of seeking redress of any grievance relating to employment and the manner in which any application should be made'. Under the Employment Relations Act 1999, the obligation to allow a worker to be accompanied has become a statutory right.

What grievance procedures are laid down in your organization? Are all your staff familiar with them?

A typical grievance procedure might have three stages in which, initially, an employee can verbally report dissatisfaction with any aspect of his or her employment to an immediate supervisor who will respond within an agreed time scale (this should be as short as possible). The supervisor is then responsible for investigating the grievance and, if possible, resolving it. If this is not possible or the employee remains dissatisfied with the outcome, he or she can state the grievance, usually in writing, to a line manager or departmental manager who will respond within an agreed time scale. If the matter remains unresolved, the line manager has to take it higher up and arrange for the employee to meet with someone more senior. If all else fails, and it is always preferable that problems are resolved internally, it may be necessary to bring in an independent third-party to resolve the grievance. This might be a representative of an employees' association, a specialist consultant or an arbitrator recommended by ACAS.

At least 20 staff of a manufacturing company in Leicester claim they have been unfairly selected for redundancy and the company is facing its second series of industrial tribunals in four years. Staff also claim that redundancy payments contradicted custom and practice in the firm. An expert in this area stated that most cases that went to industrial tribunals were the result of a failure by the company to consult staff adequately about redundancy procedures.

When one of your staff comes to you with a complaint, however trivial, you need to establish all the facts as that person reports them and check these out with other people concerned. If you try to handle problems on the basis of inadequate or incorrect information, it is quite possible for you to contribute unwittingly to making them more serious. In most cases, unless you feel you are absolutely sure of all the facts surrounding a grievance, you should avoid making any comment immediately apart from promising to investigate the complaint fully – and following this up with prompt action. Ignoring a grievance can also cause it to grow. Your aim as a manager is to investigate the underlying cause of the grievance rather than to solve the immediate problem as the individual perceives it.

According to Bouwen and Salipante (1990) there are four distinct stages through which a grievance can pass, although the time taken at each stage will vary in individual cases. The first of these is the individual's perception of dissatisfaction or private formulation of a grievance. The person feels unfairly treated or perceives an action taken by someone else as being unfair. At this stage, the individual keeps his or her dissatisfaction private. When he or she decides to talk to other people about it – public formulation – there is a transformation of the grievance and it is likely to become distorted. At this stage, the person is looking for help and support, so they put their grievance into terms that are likely to elicit this kind of response. Instead of saying 'I don't get any recognition for all this extra work I'm doing', the person may state the grievance as 'None of us gets any recognition for all this extra work' in order to get the sympathy and support of colleagues and to make their own case stronger.

After public formulation of the grievance comes the stage of action which may involve a formal or informal statement of grievance to people with authority over the situation or such actions as working to rule, decreasing productivity or the level of service, calling in trade union support and so on. Finally there will be an outcome; the grievance may be settled or it may result in some form of loss to the individual or the organization through the ruling of an industrial tribunal.

A female personnel director claimed equal pay with the male merchandising director because their work was of equal value. She tried to resolve the matter through internal grievance procedures but was turned down. After informing the company chairman that she had submitted her claim to an industrial tribunal, she went on holiday. She was dismissed on her return. The industrial tribunal awarded her 140,000 in settlement of her claim on the grounds of equal pay, sex discrimination, unfair dismissal and breach of contract.

One method of reducing the potential severity of grievance, which is becoming increasingly popular and appears to be very effective, is the creation of 'peer review committees' from among employees of the organization. The person with the grievance and his or her supervisor can select a small panel from among a pool of the employee's peers who will be responsible for listening to the grievance and suggesting ways in which it might be resolved. There is a perceived fairness in this system since most people are more prepared to accept the judgement of a selection of their peers than that of a superior or even of an external agency. It can also speed up the process whereby the grievance is given a fair hearing and this can often reduce frustration created by the feeling that no one is taking any notice.

> In a case which went to an Industrial Tribunal and an Employment Appeal Tribunal, a company changed the basis on which two salesmen were rewarded, resulting in a drop in pay. The salesmen attempted to have their grievances heard by the Managing Director and the Chairman of the company, but were unsuccessful. They eventually resigned and claimed 'constructive dismissal' – which is so termed because it arises when an employee believes the employer leaves him/her no alternative but to terminate the employment contract. The Industrial Tribunal decided that failure to use a grievance procedure amounted to breach of contract and the salesmen were able to claim damages from the company.

MANAGING DISCIPLINE

Whereas grievances are initiated by the workers, discipline is initiated by the management. Again, and possibly even more so than in the case of grievances, it necessary for a manager to tread very warily. Initiating disciplinary action should not be taken lightly.

It is unfortunate that, by association, discipline is often linked with grievance whereas the two should be considered as entirely separate activities. Employees, as you have seen, have the right to express their dissatisfaction about shortcomings and problems related to their job and working environment and should be encouraged to follow laid down grievance procedures. 'Disciplinary action' should not be considered the result of, or even connected with, any genuine grievance voiced by an employee.

As with grievance procedures, however, there is a legal obligation to provide employees with written details of disciplinary procedures within the organization. The ACAS Advisory Handbook 'Discipline and Grievances at Work' (2001), notes that it is important to look at ways of preventing disciplinary problems in the first place by following good policies in areas such as selection, induction, training, motivation, communication; by setting appropriate standards and rules in key areas such as absence, timekeeping, conduct, and performance; and also by dealing with any issues as early as possible in order to 'nip in the bud' the need to take disciplinary action. It suggests several reasons for having disciplinary rules, namely because they:

- are necessary for promoting fairness and order in the treatment of individuals and in the conduct of industrial relations;
- assist an organization to operate effectively;
- set standards of conduct at work;
- provide a fair method of dealing with alleged failures to observe the rules;
- ensure that employees know what standards are expected of them;
- are a legal requirement;
- become important in disputes about the fairness or otherwise of decisions to dismiss.

The Code of Practice, which is incorporated in the handbook and does have a legal status, suggests the following features of good disciplinary procedures. They should:

- be in writing;
- specify to whom they apply;
- be non-discriminatory;
- provide for matters to be dealt with without undue delay;
- provide for proceedings, witness statements and records to be kept confidential;
- indicate the disciplinary actions which may be taken;
- specify the levels of management which have the authority to take the various forms of disciplinary action;
- provide for workers to be informed of the complaints against them and where possible all relevant evidence before any hearing;
- provide workers with an opportunity to state their case before decisions are reached;
- provide workers with the right to be accompanied;
- ensure that – except in cases of gross misconduct – no employees are dismissed for a first breach of discipline;
- ensure that disciplinary action is not taken until the case has been carefully investigated;
- ensure that workers are given an explanation for any penalty imposed;

- provide a right of appeal – normally to a more senior manager – and specify the procedure to be followed.

Although the handbook cannot be enforced legally, failure by employers to conform to the spirit of the its contents will be noted in any subsequent action such as a claim for unfair dismissal.

A common disciplinary procedure used for all but cases of summary dismissal would include three stages. The first of these would be a verbal warning or, if the offence is more serious, a written warning which sets out the nature of the offence and what is likely to happen if it continues or if there are further offences. If there is further misconduct, a final written warning is issued which should contain a statement that any recurrence would lead to suspension or dismissal or some other penalty. If the misconduct still continues, the final stage might be a disciplinary transfer, suspension without pay or dismissal depending on the offence.

Investigate   How do your staff find out about your organization's rules and regulations?

If there is a problem which involves violation of the rules, you need to know about it as quickly as possible either through personal observation or from your supervisors. Check your facts – is the employee genuinely breaking a rule; does he or she realize this? If there does seem to be a real or potential problem, tell the employee about your concern and arrange to have a discussion about it.

At this stage, you are not invoking formal disciplinary procedures; you are trying to avoid that being necessary. You are using informal methods in an attempt to prevent the problem getting worse. In your discussion you need to find out if the employee realizes he or she is breaking organizational rules and ask them what they are going to do about it. You should point out to them the potential penalties they might incur if formal disciplinary procedures are set in motion – not as a threat but as a statement of fact. The atmosphere of this meeting should be one of trust and support rather than of criticism. Your aim is to get the employee to understand what he or she is doing wrong and for you both to agree on a solution. If this method fails and you have to invoke the procedures, accept that this is necessary not only in order to improve the situation but to maintain your own authority and credibility with your staff.

DISMISSAL

Most managers dislike having to dismiss a member of their staff with the accompanying resentment, bitterness and grief this can involve. Some avoid a termination interview by letting staff know in writing rather than in person that they are being dismissed. This is not surprising when you consider that only about 16 per cent of managers required to dismiss others have received any training in this area.

Andrew Cracknell, creative director of the advertising agency BSB Dorland, says: 'By its nature, firing someone is a tasteless converzation. You can't have a good sacking like you can't have a good funeral.' His best tip is to fire people in their own offices. 'People usually want to be left alone, and it means they don't have to stumble through the office afterwards. More selfishly, you can end the interview when you choose.'

The legislation is complex and you need to be very sure that you have good reasons for fair dismissal before embarking on the process. Any employee has the right to be given a chance to improve his or her work performance or conduct, to be given a chance to explain the reasons for his or her behaviour and to exercise the right to appeal against dismissal. Proper notice, according to the employee's contract, must be given, orally and in writing.

Geraldine Bedell (1992) has some advice for managers faced with telling someone they are going to be dismissed. She suggests:

- Writing a script beforehand to which you can refer if the situation becomes too emotional and you fear you may lose control of it.
- Rehearsing your script or whatever you are going to say.
- Choosing your time – people need to take action to find other jobs quickly and Friday afternoon is not the best time.
- Taking the telephone off the hook; avoiding interruptions.
- Trying to create a one-to-one calm atmosphere.
- Explaining, but not justifying, and avoiding recriminations.
- Setting the scene briefly, then giving the news clearly.
- Ensuring you have written details of terms you are offering and that you give the other person a copy.
- Moving quickly from giving the bad news to ways in which you can offer support.

■ Closing the meeting after about 10 minutes, although you may feel you should arrange a follow-up.
■ Writing notes on what took place.

Summary

Managers are likely to find themselves in challenging situations from time to time, and it is important that they appreciate the forces that operate in organizations and may lead to such situations, and also the need to create the procedures and institutions that may help to resolve the issues arising.

Within the area of diversity, it is important to recognize the advantages that are available from a diverse workforce, possibly with differing cultural characteristics. The underlying assumptions for managing diversity should be those of equal opportunities.

For the second cluster of issues, those of power, stress, and conflict, perhaps the key requirement for successful management is awareness of the underlying pressures, so that if at all possible difficult situations can be prevented from developing. That said, all three are integral dimensions of modern organizations, and it would be unrealistic to suggest that they can entirely prevented.

The outputs of some of these pressures can be felt through the third cluster, dealing with unions, and managing grievances and discipline. With the latter two, again prevention is better than cure, but if they do arise, it is very important that they be dealt with through appropriate procedures. ACAS and its publications is the best source to look for advice in setting up such procedures.

Activities

1 Evaluate the extent of diversity in your own area of responsibility, and write a policy for yourself to deal with it.
2 Reflect on the recent instances of conflict in your unit. How many of them were at least to some degree constructive in their outcomes? Why was this?
3 Obtain a copy of the ACAS handbook on 'Discipline and Grievances at Work'. How far does your organization live up to the content of the handbook in the way in which its procedures are laid out. Is there anything that you think ought to be changed?

CHAPTER 10

The regulation of behaviour at work

INTRODUCTION

In this chapter we deal with the implications for managing people of the legal system and the institutions which complement it. There has been a substantial increase over the last 30 years in a wide range of aspects of the impact of law on employment issues, from the scope covered to the detail involved to the numbers of times that the law has been invoked in cases before tribunals or courts. Managers frequently have to face situations which could have legal consequences; most of course do not result in any such drastic development, which is just as well if work is to have continuity and stability, but managers need to be aware of what might be involved in a situation or an action. And it cannot be overstated that the best way of avoiding any problem is for managers themselves to be aware of the principles of the law, if not the details.

Many larger organizations employ specialist staff to deal with personnel-related matters and it is their responsibility to keep up to date with the many and frequent changes in the law, particularly now that EU Directives are compounding the situation. A list of the various relevant pieces of legislation and regulations at the end of this chapter shows that this is quite a daunting task even for experts. But, even in organizations with this facility, the line manager will be involved in any formal grievance or disciplinary matters. On a day-to-day basis, you may have to deal with the first signs of trouble and, if there is no handy Personnel Department, with subsequent action. In many cases, it is the manager's responsibility to deal with cases of grievance or to become involved in disciplinary action when this becomes inevitable; it is also his or her responsibility to offer help and advice to staff who have work-related problems and, where necessary, to recommend that they seek professional advice.

The chapter will cover the following issues:

- The legal and institutional framework of employment
- Advisory, Conciliation and Arbitration Service (ACAS)
- The principles of the employment relationship
- Pay
- Discrimination
- Health and safety at work
- Unfair dismissal
- Redundancy
- Parental rights
- Working time
- The legal framework of collective bargaining
- Wider rights in the employment context

THE LEGAL AND INSTITUTIONAL FRAMEWORK OF EMPLOYMENT

Patterns of overt conflict have changed considerably in the last 20 years in Britain. There are now many less strikes and collective conflict, but the number of cases relating to individuals going to employment tribunals has risen very significantly. The law has also changed very considerably, in part to reduce the power of unions, but also to fit in with the emerging scope and importance of European legal frameworks incorporated into British law through European mechanisms. It is not expected of individuals managers that they have a detailed knowledge of law, but it is necessary for them to have a knowledge of the broad framework of an organization's legal obligations, since it is all too frequent for legal consequences to derive through ignorance from unintended behaviour, even at relatively junior levels of management. The most important institutions in British employment relations are ACAS (Advisory, Conciliation and Arbitration Service) and the employment (previously industrial) tribunals, which will now be briefly examined.

THE ADVISORY, CONCILIATION AND ARBITRATION SERVICE (ACAS)

ACAS was created in 1975 and covers the three areas its title suggests. It has come to be a trusted-third party agency which must take some of the credit for the improvement in British industrial relations. Its advisory work is perhaps the least publicized but most important part of its work and involves providing information and advice and promoting good practice. We have already mentioned the ACAS Handbook and Code of Practice for Discipline and Grievances at Work, and there are several others which provide valuable guidance to best practice in the workplace, based on the experiences of its staff and backed by the ACAS Council which represents both sides of industry. These publications are regularly updated and new issues covered; thus in 2000 a new advisory booklet was produced on changing patterns of work to provide advice on implementing part-time working, homeworking, job sharing, shift working, and annualized hours, while new leaflets were introduced on holidays and holiday pay and to respond to the rise in requests for advice on bullying and harassment. In addition, ACAS produced a more general booklet 'Towards Better Employment Relations: Using the ACAS Advisory Service' which describes the help ACAS offers and provides a series of illustrative case studies. (It is worth noting that ACAS is not the only agency which produces advisory publications – thus in 2000 the Equal Opportunities Commission, the National Disability Council and the Commission for Racial Equality published an important leaflet for small businesses 'Equal Opportunities is Your Business Too'.)

Beyond its publications ACAS provides both general and specific advice. In 2000–01 it operated 546 conferences and seminars to promote best practice and to provide information about new legal developments (such as the introduction of working time regulations in 1999), and was involved in almost 3,000 visits to workplaces and over 500 projects in companies and institutions to help management and employee representatives work together to build more effective organizations. In addition, ACAS received 760,000 enquiries for information or advice at its system of Public Enquiry Points located in its regional offices, of which 56 per cent came from individual employees. Most of these could be dealt with on the phone, but some required letters, or occasionally personal interviews. Many of these enquiries came from people, either employers or employees, in small business, who were unclear about aspects of the increasingly complex legal requirements.

The second area in which ACAS has a statutory duty is to promote settlement of a wide range of employment rights complaints which have been or could be made to an employment tribunal. This is called individual conciliation, and much of this work is handled on the phone by ACAS staff. In 2000–01 there were 167,186 complaints leading to 42,967 (or 25.7 per cent) cases going to employment tribunals. This is a very substantial increase on the figure 20 years earlier, when there were 46,447 complaints, of which 12,929 (or 30 per cent) went forward to tribunals. Thus there were almost four times as many complaints, and some two and a half times as many tribunal cases. Unfair dismissal is, as it was in 1980, the most likely cause of an individual making a complaint, but these only amounted to less than a third of the total in 2000–01, as compared to 90 per cent in 1980. Table 10.1 indicates the breakdown and disposal of cases going to conciliation in 2000–01:

Table 10.1
Individual Conciliation by ACAS, 2000–01

Type	Cases Received	Settled	Withdrawn	Tribunal
Unfair dismissal	50,065	24,340	11,965	14,977
Protection of wages	39,464	13,403	11,058	10,106
Equal pay	4,933	614	834	190
Breach of contract	29,390	11,288	7,398	8,139
Sex discrimination	9,082	3,021	1,900	1,206
Race discrimination	4,153	1,322	1,303	1,041
Disability	4,422	1,647	1,102	679
Other	25,677	8,498	5,920	6,629
Total	167,186	64,133	41,480	42,967

Of the total number of cases not going to a tribunal, some 38 per cent were settled by ACAS conciliation and 25 per cent were withdrawn, a proportion of which is also due to ACAS conciliation. Many of the complaints lead as a point of referral to other types of help that ACAS can give in developing good practice at work, illustrating the inter-related nature of ACAS's activities. A recent dimension of this is the capacity for certain employment tribunal cases to be handled by arbitration. This possibility was introduced in May 2001 as a result of the growing time, cost and, in some cases, publicity attached to the handling of unfair dismissal cases through employment tribunals, but as yet there is no indication about the uptake of this opportunity.

This leads us to the third aspect of ACAS responsibilities, that of collective dispute conciliation and resolution. The number of requests for collective conciliation was 1,472 in 2000–01 (as compared to 1910 in 1980), and the success rate was 90 per cent, a tribute to ACAS's impartiality and its experience over the last 25 years. Half the cases dealt with pay and/or other terms and conditions, with the next most important being trade union recognition with 22 per cent. The final stage of this side of ACAS activity is arbitration or dispute mediation, and in 2000–01 there were 62 cases, of which one was mediation. This is a much smaller number than in the first few years of the life of ACAS (322 in 1980). Arbitration is a situation where the parties must agree to accept the decision of the independent arbitrator drawn from the ACAS panel of experts, although this is not strictly legally binding, and dispute mediation is where the parties are provided with a recommended solution. But there is also advisory mediation, where ACAS (rather than an independent mediator) helps the parties work together in resolving problems at work; there were 595 such cases completed in 1999–2000.

ACAS conciliated in a dispute between the Critchley Group and the National Communications Union (NCU) when the company sought to make changes in employees' terms and conditions of employment as well as trying to change the culture of the business. It gave NCU three months' notice of the termination of its recognition agreement and the union planned a series of one- and two-day strikes as a result. Following conciliation meetings with ACAS, a new recognition agreement was drawn up and revised terms and conditions were to be discussed.

EMPLOYMENT TRIBUNALS AND COURTS

Employment tribunals were first created as industrial tribunals in 1964, but their name was changed to employment tribunals by the Employment Rights Act of 1998. Normally the tribunals consist of a legally qualified chairperson and two lay members reflecting on the one hand nominations by employer organizations and on the other employee organizations. However, the lay members are not expected to represent the interests of their nominating organizations. Hearings are expected to be relatively informal, but concern at increasing legalism and bureaucracy has led the arbitration alternative mentioned earlier through ACAS. An employment tribunal is required to follow the decisions of higher courts, which comprise the Employment Appeal Tribunal (EAT), the Court of Appeal and the House of Lords. In turn all British courts must follow the guidance given by the European Court of Justice (ECJ); when a British court or tribunal decides that clarification of European law is necessary for it to make a decision, it will remit the matter to the ECJ. The European Union can create various types of legislation, the most important being regulations and directives. Regulations are generally of a broad nature and are directly applicable to all member states. Directives are instruments which require member states to translate the contents of the directive into national law and they are given two or three years to implement this. National courts also have an obligation to interpret national law in such a way that it gives effect to EU law.

THE PRINCIPLES OF THE EMPLOYMENT RELATIONSHIP

We now move to the scope of law and legislation. There is an element of common law in the concept of the contract of employment, which can be entered into informally even though a considerable degree of formality is desirable because of the consequences of having an employee. It is in fact very important that all the relevant terms and conditions are clearly understood at the time employment commences; nevertheless a lot of the practical and legal difficulties and lack of clarity which give rise to so many enquiries to ACAS is due to these issues not being sorted out at the point of employment. This is in spite of the fact that there is a legal obligation to provide a statement of particulars not later than two months after the start of employment, and these include: the identity of the parties; the date of employment, the rate of payment and the intervals at which it will be paid, any conditions relating to hours of work, holidays and holiday pay, incapacity to work through sickness or injury, the length of notice, the job title or brief description of the work to be done, any collective agreements affecting the employment, and grievance and disciplinary rules and procedures. The statement of particulars is not the whole of the contract of employment, however, and some of it may be informal and based on custom and practice. Terms may also be derived from collective agreements, works rules and statute law as well as those aspects individually determined. Changes cannot be made to a contract of employment without the consent of the employee, but the employee may be deemed to have agreed to the change if he or she does not explicitly reject it.

The existence of a contract of employment imposes certain obligations on both the employer and the employee, the breaking of which constitutes a breach of the contract of employment. These are based on both long-established common law principles and more recent statutory developments. The main duties of the employer are:

- ■ To pay wages.
- ■ To provide work, although employees who receive their full contractual remuneration cannot normally complain if they are idle.
- ■ To co-operate with the employee. This has been interpreted to mean that the employer must not upset the mutual trust on which co-operation is based, although each case must be determined on the facts.
- ■ To take reasonable care of the employee. This is both a general duty and one which involves various statutes in the health and safety area.
- ■ To provide references, although strictly speaking this refers to ex-employees.

Employees also have duties, as listed below:

- ■ To co-operate with the employer, especially the duty to obey lawful and reasonable orders and not to impede the employer's business.
- ■ To be loyal, such that the employee's own interests should not conflict with the duty they owe the employer; in particular the duty not to compete with the employer and the duty not to disclose confidential information.

■ To take reasonable care. If they do not, there is an implied duty to indemnify the employer against the consequences of their negligence.

In a case reported in 2002, Lister v. Hedley Hall, the House of Lords revolutionized the concept of vicarious liability by focusing on the closeness of the connection between the employee's job and the wrongdoing. On this basis the employers of a school warden could be liable for his sexual assaults on schoolchildren because he was employed to look after them. It did not matter that what he had done was outside what he was authorized by his employers to do.

We now move to the more specific areas of employment law.

PAY

Pay is normally settled by express terms of the contract of employment, but the Equal Pay Act of 1970 established obligations for equality of pay and the National Minimum Wage act of 1998 established a minimum wage; initially this was £3.60 per hour for adults with lower rates for younger workers, but this has now been increased (October 2001) to £4.10.

Employers must give their employees itemized pay statements.

Deductions from wages are unlawful unless approved by statute or by agreement with the employee.

Employers are responsible for paying statutory sick pay for up to 28 weeks of absence in a single period of entitlement. A right to sick pay may be inferred in the contract of employment by custom and practice or the knowledge of the parties when the contract was originated. Notification of absence must be given to the employer in accordance with rules laid down for employees.

Employers are obliged to keep records showing the amount paid to each employee.

DISCRIMINATION

There are several key pieces of legislation dealing with discrimination, including the Equal Pay act 1970, the Sex Discrimination Act 1975, the Race Relations Act 1976 and the Disability Discrimination Act of 1995. Discrimination on grounds of membership or non-membership of a trade union is also unlawful under the Trade Union and Labour Relations (Consolidation) Act 1992. Discrimination on grounds of age is not unlawful, but is discouraged by a 1999 government Code of Practice which also makes recommendations for good practice by employers. It is expected that anti-ageism legislation will be brought forward by the British government, especially in the light of the changing demographic balance. Many other countries have already abolished mandatory retirement ages.

Both the Equal Opportunities Commission and the Commission for Racial Equality have issued Codes of Practice to eliminate discrimination.

Direct discrimination occurs when on the grounds of sex, marital status or race a person is treated less favourably than another person not of that grouping would be treated. This includes cases of harassment.

> 'You should never underestimate how hard it is for anyone to complain about sexual harassment because of the embarrassment. It's often harder for men to complain than women, because of their social conditioning. It's harder again for people to complain about homosexual harassment.' (David Crew, Manager, Equal Opportunities Dept., Midland Bank, July 1995)

Indirect discrimination occurs when an employer applies a requirement or condition which would apply equally to all groups but which is such that the proportion of people from a particular grouping who can comply with it is considerably smaller than that of persons from another grouping.

In recruitment and selection, it is unlawful to discriminate in the arrangements made for recruitment, in the terms offered, or by refusing to offer employment. A wide range of practices could be problematic, from the wording of advertisements to word of mouth only recruitment or refusing to employ those who live in a particular geographical area.

Nevertheless, discrimination can be lawful in certain circumstances, such as where sex or race is a genuine occupational qualification or where discrimination is necessary in order to comply with a statute, such as in the health and safety area.

Within employment, discrimination is not permitted in respect of any opportunities for training or promotion, or any benefits or facilities.

As might be expected, discrimination is also not permitted in the area of dismissal, for whatever reason.

> A black head chef was awarded £20,634 after an industrial tribunal found that he had been sacked because of his race. The chef, who was of Nigerian origin, was dismissed following a take-over of the restaurant where he worked in Chelsea. The chef, who had an unblemished record, received no warning of his dismissal and the company who had taken over the restaurant refused to supply him with a reference.

Both employers and individuals may be sued. Individuals are liable for performing or putting pressure on someone to perform an unlawful act. Employers are not only liable directly, but also for the actions of their employees, even if the actions were done without the employer's knowledge or approval unless the employer had taken all reasonably practical steps to prevent them.

> Denise alleged that the store manager had made sexual gestures to her when they were alone. Another female employee made similar complaints. They complained to more senior management but no investigation occurred until, on union advice, written complaints were sent to their regional manager. Eventually all were interviewed. The manager remained at work during this time. He was told to apologize and Denise was offered a transfer. This was sex discrimination since there was a case of clear harassment, there had been a very slow response during which time the victim was left at work, and she, not the harasser, was expected to move. The employer was liable as the manager was exercising his supervisory duties when he harassed Denise. An employment tribunal awarded compenzation of £3,500 to Denise for injured feelings.

Since it is unusual to find evidence of direct discrimination, a case will usually depend on what inferences it is proper to draw from the facts uncovered at the tribunal.

Under the Equal Pay Act, an equality clause operates when a person is employed on 'like work' to a person of the opposite sex in the same employment. The concept of like work is focused on the job rather than the person performing it. It is for the employer to show that any differences in pay are due to a genuine material difference not related to the sex of either employee.

In a case concerning equal pay brought against North Yorkshire County Council, the Law Lords ruled that women should receive the same rate as men. The Council had argued that it needed to compete with private contractors in a competitive tendering process and the only way it could do this effectively was to pay the women at lower rates. The Law Lords' decision was particularly important in a prevailing climate where services are increasingly being contracted-out and pressures to reduce costs remain intense (ACAS, 1995).

The Disability Discrimination Act makes it unlawful for all but very small employers to discriminate against existing or potential employees for reasons relating to their disability. A disability is defined as an impairment which has a substantial and long-term adverse effect on an ability to carry out normal day-to-day activities.

Other Acts which support this policy of equal opportunities include the Pensions Act 1995 (equal access to membership of company pension schemes) and the Employment Protection (Part-time Employees) Regulations 1995 which gives part-time employees the same rights as full-timers in a range of employment protection jurisdictions.

HEALTH AND SAFETY AT WORK

The main statute in this area is the Health and Safety at Work Act 1974, and the Management of Health and Safety at Work Regulations 1992 make more explicit what the employer is required to do to manage health and safety under the Act. Both apply to every work activity, and furthermore seek to protect those outside the work context from health and safety risks arising out of work. A breach of the law or regulations amounts to a criminal act. The Health and Safety Commission or Executive can provide guidance, codes of practice, and regulations.

Every employer with five or more employees must prepare a written statement of policy on health and safety at work and the arrangements for carrying out that policy. Employers must also distribute leaflets or display posters about the requirements of health and safety law. They must also conduct a risk assessment to identify what needs to be done to comply with legal requirements.

Employers must also consult employees and their representatives, who may be trade union appointed or directly elected. The representatives can call for the setting up of a safety committee at the place of work, and it is recommended that they should given time off with pay to undertake training in the safety area. As an employer, it is necessary to provide:

- a safe place of work;
- a safe means of access to the place of work;
- a safe system of work;
- adequate materials;
- competent fellow employees;
- protection from unnecessary risk of injury;
- a safety policy;
- adequate instruction and training;
- a safety committee if union appointed safety representatives ask for one.

Certain accidents, incidents or injuries must be reported if they occur in connection with work.

UNFAIR DISMISSAL

This is the best-known and in some respects the most important part of employment law. The basic framework of legislation dates from 1970, but has been modified and consolidated, most recently in the Trade Union and Labour Relations (Consolidation) Act 1992, the Employment Rights Act 1996, and the Employment Relations Act 1999.

Every employee has the right not to be unfairly dismissed, but there are various qualifications and exclusions, in particular the need to have one year's continuous service and to be under normal retirement age.

An employee is treated as dismissed if the contract of employment is terminated by the employer with or without notice, a fixed-term contract comes to an end, or the employee terminates the contract as a result of the employer's conduct. This latter is known as constructive dismissal, and requires that the employer has breached the central tenets of the contract of employment.

In making a complaint, the employee must show that he or she was dismissed. The effective date of termination of employment is the date on which notice expires or on which termination otherwise takes effect.

Once dismissal is accepted, the burden is on the employer to show the reason, or principal reason, for the dismissal, and for the dismissal to be fair, it must fall within one of five categories:

- The capacity or qualifications of the employee for performing work of the type for which the employee was employed.
- The conduct of the employee.
- The employee was redundant.
- The employee could not continue to work without a statutory contravention being involved.
- Some other substantial reason.

Each of these potentially fair reasons is a complex area of law in its own right as the reasons have been interpreted and created precedents.

There is also a range of circumstances in which dismissal will automatically be unfair, including the assertion of a statutory right, various family reasons including pregnancy, aspects of health and safety law, and trade union membership or non-membership.

The key decision to be made by the tribunal is about reasonableness in the circumstances. More specifically, 'the determination of the question whether the dismissal was fair or unfair

(a) depends on whether in the circumstances (including the size and administrative resources of the employer's undertaking) the employer acted reasonably or unreasonably in treating it as a sufficient reason for dismissing the employee, and

(b) shall be determined in accordance with equity and the substantial merits of the case.'

Employers will be expected to treat employees in similar circumstances in a similar way. Nevertheless, each case will be decided on its own facts and with the capacity to consider both mitigating circumstances and aggravating factors.

Employees cannot claim unfairness if they are dismissed while taking part in unofficial industrial action.

Procedural fairness is important as well as substantive fairness. The ACAS Code of Practice of Disciplinary and Grievance Procedures (revised 2000), key parts of which were outlined in Chapter 9, is a substantial consideration here. While it does not have the force of law, it will weigh heavily against an employer if it is not followed. Natural justice is an important feature of procedural fairness. An accused person should know the case against them and be able to dispute it and should be able to request that they are accompanied by a companion, whether a union official or a friend.

Tribunals have a number of possible findings in dismissal situations. They can find the dismissal to be fair, or they can find it to be unfair, in which case there are three main alternative remedies. These are reinstatement, re-engagement, and compenzation. The first two remedies are relatively rare, and are dependent on the dismissed employee wanting re-employment and the practicality of such an order.

Compenzation usually consists of a basic award and a compensatory award. The basic award is calculated in the same way as a redundancy payment (see below), while a compensatory award is what the tribunal 'considers just and equitable in all the circumstances having regard to the loss sustained by the complainant in consequence of the dismissal insofar as that loss is attributable to action taken by the employer'. The maximum amount of a compensatory award was raised considerably in the Employment Relations Act 1999 to £50,000 and is now increased according to the retail price index. It is up to the complainant to prove the loss, which is defined under a number of headings. Some of these, such as loss of pension rights, can be very complex calculations.

Other important dimensions of calculating compenzation for unfair dismissal and redundancy are continuity of employment, normal working hours, and a week's pay, each of which has legal implications. Thus normal working hours are those required by the contract of employment and do not include non-contractual overtime, while a week's pay is the gross amount payable for a week under the contract of employment.

REDUNDANCY

Redundancy is a potentially fair reason for dismissal, but it carries a number of important dimensions of its own. Redundancy is defined as where the employer has or will have a diminution of the requirement of work of a particular kind.

The burden of proof is on the employer to show that any offer of alternative employment was suitable and rejection by the employee was unreasonable. There may be a trial period to consider offers of alternative employment.

The employer should give as much warning as possible to enable the employees or the unions to consider possible alternatives or seek alternative work. There are specific consultation requirements where an employer is proposing to make redundant 20 or more employees in an establishment in a period of 90 days or less.

Calculating redundancy payments is based on the following formula: one and a half weeks' pay for each year of employment in which the employee is aged between 41 and 64; one week's pay for each year of employment in which the individual was aged between 22 and 40; and half a week's pay for each year of employment between 18 and 21.

British Aerospace made 500 workers redundant out of their workforce of 7,000. Workers were assessed against six criteria and marked on one of four grades. The points were added up and those with the lowest scores were made redundant. Of those involved, 234 complained of unfair selection for redundancy, mainly on grounds of lack of consultation and unfairness in the selection procedure.

Selection for redundancy can be a minefield of legal requirements as can be seen from the examples above. The main requirements for fair dismissal for redundancy are as follows:

- The redundancy is genuine and is not being claimed by the employer as the reason for dismissing an incompetent employee.
- The people selected for redundancy have been chosen on the basis of agreed criteria, which may be criteria agreed within the company or in agreement with the trade union.
- Elected employee representatives or independent trade unions have been consulted.
- There is no suitable alternative work available; the organization is required to try to find alternative work for employees rather than declare them redundant.
- Redundancy selection does not contravene the Sex Discrimination, Race Discrimination or Disability Discrimination Acts.

PARENTAL RIGHTS

A pregnant woman is entitled to paid time off for antenatal care. It is automatically unfair to dismiss a woman by reason of her pregnancy.

Maternity leave is divided into ordinary (up to 18 weeks), compulsory (not less than two weeks after childbirth, included in the ordinary leave period), and additional (up to 29 weeks after childbirth) leave periods. Statutory maternity pay is available for a maximum of eight weeks. A woman is entitled to return to her job under the original contract of employment and on terms and conditions not less favourable than would have occurred had she not been absent.

Parental leave is available for parents who have responsibility for a child. The employee is entitled to 13 weeks in respect of each child, but the leave cannot be taken in periods of less than a week or for more than four weeks in any one year. This leave may be postponed by the employer for up to six months.

Employees are also entitled to take reasonable time off for incidents involving a dependant.

Transfer of undertakings regulations were introduced in 1981 as a result of the European Acquired Rights Directive. They are intended to protect the contract of employment and the employment relationship when the undertaking is transferred from one employer to another. The issue of when a transfer occurs is however a complex one. All rights claims and liabilities, with the exception of pension rights, are transferred, including non-contractual rights.

In the Nicholas case it was held that liability for an act of sex discrimination transferred from the transferor company to the tranferee company.

WORKING TIME

The Working Time Regulations of 1998 implement the European Working Time Directive and provide for a maximum 48 hour week during a 17 week reference period, and also provide rules on night work, rest periods and annual leave.

The individual worker is able to opt out of the 48 hour week and there is provision determining the rules by collective agreements.

Employees who are officials of unions recognized by the employer are entitled to paid time off during working hours for trade union activities. Employees are entitled to be permitted time off without pay for a number of public duties such as local authorities.

Young employees who are not receiving full-time education are entitled to time off to study for certain qualifications.

Someone who has been employed for two years or more and is under notice of dismissal is entitled to reasonable time off during working hours to look for new work.

THE LEGAL FRAMEWORK OF COLLECTIVE BARGAINING

This has been a highly controversial area in British industrial history, and the legislation governing it has been subject to considerable change in the last quarter of a century.

A trade union must be certified as independent by the Certification Officer and must be recognized by an employer in order to enjoy legal privileges in the area of collective bargaining. Establishing an appropriate bargaining unit is a key prerequisite for the recognition procedure and is carried out by the Central Arbitration Committee (CAC), which also determines whether the union has the support of a majority of workers within the bargaining unit. The CAC can also be used for a procedure of de-recognition, and for enforcing the disclosure of information for collective bargaining.

Collective agreements are not generally enforceable and indeed are conclusively presumed not to have been intended by the parties to be legally enforceable contracts unless the agreement is in writing and contains a provision which states that the parties intend it to be enforceable.

All forms of industrial action are likely to constitute a breach of an individual's contract of employment. Inducing the breach of a contract, whether of employment or commercial, is a key dimension of the law on industrial action. However, there is statutory immunity against tort challenges where the industrial action takes place in contemplation or furtherance of a trade dispute. Unions and their officials can benefit from immunity only if the union has authorized the industrial action after there has been majority support for the action in a ballot of the members concerned not more than four weeks before the start of the action.

Other actions with possible legal consequences include picketing, intimidation, conspiracy, inducing a breach of a statutory duty, and interference with business by unlawful means.

There are now also substantial legal controls on the relationship between trade unions and their members.

WIDER RIGHTS IN THE EMPLOYMENT CONTEXT

The Human Rights Act 1998 incorporates Article 8(1) of the European Convention on Human Rights. Areas which may have an influence on employment law are the right to respect for private and family life, freedom of thought, conscience and religion, freedom of expression, and freedom of assembly and association.

The Data Protection Act 1998 also arose from European sources and provides protection against misuse of personal information by giving rights to individuals about whom information is recorded on computers.

The Access to Medical Reports Act 1988 provides a right of access to any medical report relating to an individual which has been or will be supplied by a medical practitioner for employment or insurance purposes. Nevertheless medical practitioners who carry out such assessments owe a duty of care to the employer who is relying on the report rather than to the employee.

Rehabilitation of Offenders Act 1974. Where a person who has been convicted of an offence and has served a sentence in custody, after a period of between five and 10 years, he/she must be treated as if the offence had never been committed. This means that the candidate is not obliged to reveal any such sentence to a prospective employer. Certain categories of employee, including accountants, lawyers, teachers, those in the medical profession and those who work with persons under the age of 18 can be asked to disclose any previous offences.

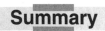

Summary

The law now plays a much bigger part in employment relationships than it did for most of last century, and moreover, there has both been a substantial amount of change in existing law, and a good deal of new law, much of it originating in Europe.

The most important move has been a transition from a primary focus on collective issues and behaviour in industrial conflict to developing the rights of the individual worker. Not only have these latter rights been extended, but there has been a continuous growth in the number of cases being taken to ACAS conciliation and the employment tribunals.

Another dimension is that the law has become more complex and based on precedent, rather than being decided on general industrial relations principles as was originally intended when the tribunals were first set up.

Unfair dismissal is still the most important issue for the tribunals, but it is now much less dominant as other types of case have become more numerous.

Procedural aspects of employer process, together with consistency of behaviour and policy application, are important dimensions in decisions, as well as the factual circumstances.

Activities

1   Bring together the organization's range of rules for all the areas which may have legal consequences under employment law, so that you are aware of their existence if you need to refer to them.

The relevant Acts for the material in this chapter are:

- Employment Protection Act 1975
- Employment Protection (Consolidation) Act 1978
- Trade Union and Labour Relations (Consolidation) Act 1992
- Employment Rights Act 1996
- Employment Rights Act 1998
- Employment Relations Act 1999
- Sex Discrimination Acts 1975 and 1986
- Race Relations Act 1976
- Disability Discrimination Act 1995
- Equal Pay Act 1970 and Equal Pay (Amendment) Regulations 1983
- Health and Safety at Work Act 1974
- Wages Act 1986
- Pensions Act 1995
- Human Rights Act 1998
- Data Protection Act 1998
- Access to Medical Reports Act 1988
- Rehabilitation of Offenders Act 1974
- Management of Health and Safety at Work Regulations 1992
- Employment Protection (Part-time Employees) Regulations 1995
- Collective Redundancies and Transfer of Undertakings (Protection of Employment) (Amendment) Regulations 1999
- Working Time Regulations 1999

CHAPTER 11

Managing in a changing world

INTRODUCTION

'In today's increasingly uncertain, competitive and fast-moving world, companies must rely more and more on individuals to come up with new ideas, to develop creative responses and push for changes before opportunities disappear or minor irritants turn into catastrophes. Innovations, whether in products, market strategies, technological processes or work practices, are designed not by machines but by people.' (Moss Kanter, 1992)

'Organizations are never static: something about them is always changing. For example, there is turnover in the membership, new administrative procedures are introduced, or a new customer arrives on the scene. None of these events is completely self contained; each has implications for other aspects of organizational life. Some of them obviously result from decisions made within the organization, some of them originate with decisions outside, and others just seem to happen. The common factor is that when something changes, whether or not it has been planned or decided by organizational members, it will have repercussive effects which will be variously welcomed, discarded or ignored by people within and outside the organization. Their reactions will in turn affect other things.' (Dawson, 1992)

You will recall that we began this book by introducing the theme of change, and gave a substantial range of dimensions in which change is taking place. Indeed, most of this book has been about managing change of one sort or another – recruiting new staff, looking at innovative ways in which people's jobs can be changed and improved, managing changes in individual and group behaviour, managing the changing processes which teams go through, managing people's development, coping with changes in people's working lives. Writers on organizational change see it as essential if organizations and the people who work in them are to grow and develop or even keep up with the competition. It is therefore appropriate that this concluding chapter deals more explicitly with the challenge of change and how it can be managed.

Coping with change means that organizations can no longer expect stability. If its major customer goes out of business or takes its custom elsewhere or a new competitor enters the market, the organization's financial situation can plummet overnight. For managers, it means keeping a close eye on productivity and performance and, too often, having to manage organizational restructuring.

Although some people see change as a challenge and an opportunity, others fear it. They see change as threatening because organizational change, however small, usually involves people in changing their existing working practices and processes and even their attitudes towards the job and others in the organization. And often they are right to fear it. There is hardly a significant organization which has not undergone substantial change in the last decade. The repercussions, moreover, have often been very painful. Consider the different words and phrases which are used to describe restructuring – hard words such as downsizing, delayering, headcount reduction, terminating employment, redundancy – even though the official front is all about valuing contributions, counselling and relocating. This does not mean that change is undesirable or unnecessary, but it does mean that it is not easy when it can substantially affect people's lives.

As a manager, you have a choice. The choice is not between managing change or not managing change but between managing change through people or despite people. In virtually every case, the former is more successful.

'Things aren't going to be the same when the merger happens. Demos is going to be the dominant partner because it is very hierarchical – very structured with strong financial controls. We're big, but very decentralized. Each of the business units do things their own way – lots of autonomy although they are supported from Head Office. We're losing 100 staff here but Demos employees will come in with a completely different cultural background. I can see all the good work we've done over the last few years being lost as well.' (manager in pharmaceuticals company)

Your role in change will depend on your role in the organization. For junior or first-line managers, change is often imposed from higher up in the organization and they have to manage the process; even so, this can be a difficult job, requiring real leadership skills. Change does not just happen because those above give an order. Moreover, there may well be changes which need initiating at a relatively low level. Nevertheless, for more senior managers, there is generally more of an opportunity to contribute to the planning of change.

In this chapter, we include:

- Pressures for change.
- Challenges in change.
- Levels of change.
- Initiating and planning for change.
- Stages of change.
- Responses to change.

PRESSURES FOR CHANGE

Pressures for change usually come from outside the organization in the first place, from changes in the organization's environment. Some can be identified quite a long way ahead, such as demographic changes, while others come out of the blue, as literally happened in the September 2001 attacks on the World Trade Centre in New York and its impact on the world economy. These external pressures can combine with pressures from inside the organization, such as the need to increase productivity or improve performance or the need to improve working conditions. Although both will be considered separately here, they are nearly always interlinked.

External pressures for change

The rapidly changing environment in which organizations exist in today's world creates continuous pressure from change. These pressures can be categorized as social, technological, political, economic, environmental and market-related, as shown in Figure 11.1. Many general trends and pressures in these areas were identified in Chapter 1, but many others will be more specific to industries or even individual organizations.

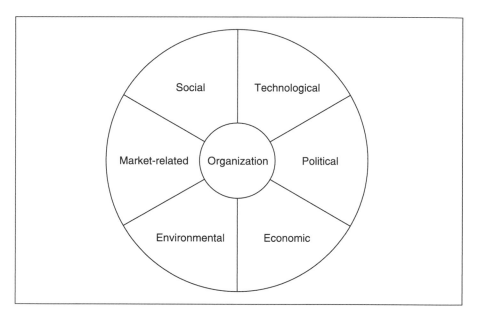

Figure 11.1
External pressures
for change

In Russia and other parts of Eastern Europe, subsidized canteens and free meat supplies used to be the top priorities for workers in Western-owned companies. These have now been overtaken by low-interest loans, personal credit cards, car allowances and medical benefits.

At its 33rd World Santa Claus and Christmas Elves Congress, held in Copenhagen this month, delegates debated the ethics of the Internet and learned how to set up their own Web sites. 'We have to see the new technology as an opportunity', said Ib Rasmussen, organizer of the Congress. 'We have to say to children that there is not one single Father Christmas, but a well-organized staff of Santas and elves.' (*The Guardian*, 22 July 1996)

'I handed the English typescript of Megatrends Asia to my Chinese business partner . . . within 19 days it had been translated into Mandarin and 200,000 copies were in circulation.' (John Naisbitt, honorary Professor, Nanjing University)

Two employees of ICI won an award from the company after they had persuaded it to set up an ecology team. Now all ICI sites have a policy to conserve and enhance wildlife in the area.

Investigate

Take each of the eight areas in Figure 11.1, and identify a pressure that has had an impact on your organization. How have they affected your job and those of your staff?

Internal pressures for change

Pressures for change from within an organization can be 'top-down' or 'bottom-up'; that is, they can come from the leader of the organization or senior management or from the organization's employees.

If you are relatively junior in your organization, you have probably experienced top-down change. Your reaction to it will have depended on how it was communicated to you, how closely it affected you personally and whether you were consulted about the change and its effects at any point. Except in times of real crisis, top-down change is usually resented by those it affects lower down in the organization.

Top-down change needs to be handled sensitively and involve as many people as possible lower down in the organization if it is going to be accepted without resistance. Channels of communication, upward and downward, need to be effective and staff need to be kept informed about plans for change. Where time and other pressures allow, as much consultation as is possible about the way the change will be implemented and its effects on individuals and groups will result in a higher rate of acceptance and even positive enthusiasm.

Radical change, whether as a result of external or internal pressures or a combination of these, often has to be imposed from the top when a Chief Executive or management team is charged with turning around a failing organization.

Radical change is usually engendered by strong external pressures and the likelihood of collapse unless drastic action is taken. It usually involves large-scale redundancies or relocation of staff and will only be successful if senior management is committed to the strategy and staff are kept informed of what is happening.

In 1995, Mobil Oil moved their London office to Milton Keynes. Within 24 hours of the announcement of the relocation in November 1994, employees were given a presentation by senior management explaining the benefits of the move. The following day, a Saturday, a video package arrived at each employee's home showing the new offices and the Milton Keynes area. Consultants were brought in and visited individual staff to discuss the problems they faced including the selling of their property. Home owners who agreed to move were offered a guaranteed price by the consultants who then took over the responsibility for selling the property. Half of the employees agreed to relocate and 60 per cent of these moved to the Milton Keynes area. Those who chose not to relocate received redundancy payments and full outplacement support. (Merrick, 1995)

Pressure from staff can be very effective in creating change, providing senior management are prepared to take notice. If ignored, it can degenerate into dissatisfaction and even result in industrial action.

Employees at Howard's Dairies had petitioned for longer rest periods for some time, but their arguments were ignored. Eventually, their grievance reached the level where the union was brought in and a long and bitter battle with the employers was fought before going to arbitration. The arbitrator found for the employees and the company was forced to increase rest times accordingly. However, since the dispute had involved the staff in working to rule over a period of several weeks, the company had lost several major customers during this time and its financial outlook was bleak.

Investigate What do you think might have been the pressures for change underlying both the Mobil Oil and Howard's Dairies cases?

THE CHALLENGES IN CHANGE

Investigate Think about your own reactions to change and jot down the words you would use to describe recent changes at work and the way you feel about them.

You may have used words like 'exhilarating', 'exciting', 'challenging' or you may have used others such as 'frightening', 'exhausting', 'unnecessary'. In fact, many people feel very threatened by change as you saw from the example in the Introduction. People who have been made redundant can usually blame this on some kind of change – a change in working practices, in company structure, in market demand and so on. People who are stuck somewhere in the middle of an organization can blame this on not having the right skills at the right time – being 'too old to learn new tricks'. And, too often, change takes place without the involvement of many of those affected by it, creating fear and suspicion of the unknown.

We have to accept that change is inevitable in today's world. As you saw in Chapter 1, organizations are changing all the time and managers and others need different skills to meet the challenges of these changes.

Investigate Can you think of some of the opportunities that change can offer to those who are involved in it at work?

You may have experienced some of these opportunities yourself. The chance to learn new skills, for example, and working with new people and new technology. Job satisfaction may be increased through improved working conditions and practices and better, more efficient use of your skills and time. New or changed jobs can bring increased status and responsibility; reward systems can be improved and made more relevant. Even though being made redundant may be traumatic at the time, it may seem in retrospect, it may have forced you to accept the reality of the situation and change yourself for the better (although it must be noted that for many people who are made redundant there are no second chances).

With all these pressures on organizations to change, you would expect there to be other factors which constrain change from taking place. This, of course, is true. Factors which limit change and can prevent it from occurring could include financial or other resource constraints, people's attitudes and resistance to change and legal or other restrictions. The psychologist Kurt Lewin devised a model which has been called 'forcefield analysis' as a way of looking at change situations (Figure 11.2).

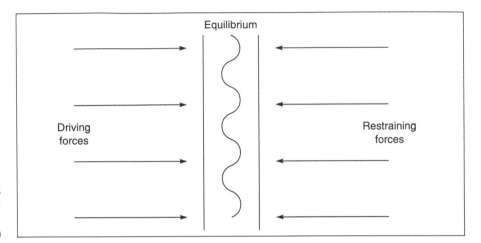

Figure 11.2
Forcefield analysis
(adapted from
Lewin, 1951)

Pressures for change, Lewin called 'driving forces'; these included any external or internal pressures but might also include individuals or groups of people. 'Restraining forces' are Lewin's term for factors which are preventing change from taking place and these too can include individuals or groups. When the driving and restraining forces for change are equal, then a state of equilibrium exists – in other words, nothing happens. If the relative strengths of either the driving or restraining forces change, then there is activity, which may consist either of change or of a deeper entrenchment into preserving the status quo. By varying the width of the arrows representing the forces, as in Figure 11.3, relative strengths can be assessed. In any situation, each of the arrows would have a title that described the individual driving or restraining force.

You need to identify the driving and restraining forces of any change you are proposing to make in order to analyse how successful – or otherwise – it may be. If you find that the restraining forces are equal to, or stronger than, the driving forces, you will need to strengthen the driving forces. This could be accomplished by providing more resources, financial or human, to add to the driving forces you have already identified. It could also, and often more easily, be achieved by reducing the strength of the restraining forces. You could, for example, decrease fear of change as a restraining force

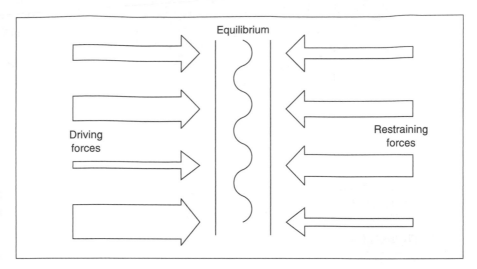

Figure 11.3
Assessing the
relative strengths
of driving and
restraining forces

by involving people in the plans for change and reducing their level of anxiety about its outcome.

Investigate

Take the pressures for change that you identified in the Mobil Oil and Howard's Dairies cases above. Now add the pressures against change and set them against each other in a forcefield analysis, drawing lines of what you consider to be the appropriate thickness.

LEVELS OF CHANGE

The length of time needed for managing change and the degree of difficulty you should expect are both directly related to the level of the change which is being proposed, as shown in Figure 11.4. Changes can be made at the individual, group and organizational levels and a change which affects a single individual can be expected to be simpler to manage and to take less time than one which affects groups of people or the whole organization. This is, however, rather simplistic since making a small change to the job of one individual can quite often affect others. For example, if I changed from giving work to my secretary in manuscript to dictating it, her method of work would change but the effect would probably be restricted to her alone. If, however, I asked her to work from home, such a change would involve others in supplying her with appropriate

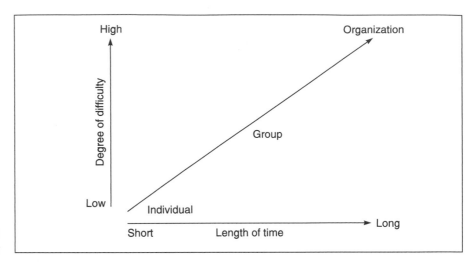

Figure 11.4
Levels of change

equipment, making arrangements for cover for my telephone calls when I was absent and, probably, widespread reactions from other secretarial and clerical staff concerning their working conditions; the level of the change would not be at the individual level but at the group and, even possibly, the organizational levels. A major consideration in planning change is to identify its effects at all levels before putting it into practice.

Investigate   Think of a change in which you have been involved – was it initiated at the individual, group or organizational level?

INITIATING AND PLANNING FOR CHANGE

One of the most difficult but nevertheless most important dimensions of change is to decide when it is desirable and how it should be achieved and then planning for its introduction. It is possible that a very sudden event, such as the attacks on the World Trade Centre, imposes change, or alternatively that change slowly evolves, almost without anybody noticing it. But these two extremes are exceptional. In the vast majority of cases change results from decisions that it is desirable, and somebody initiates the process. Even if the process of change is highly consultative, somebody usually has to begin it, and if, which again is the norm, that person is a manager, it helps greatly that a good deal of analysis and preparation predates any proposals. There are arguably five separate issues that need to be considered:

212

- Define the problem. Is the change really necessary, or at least desirable? Change for the sake of it, as sometimes seems to employees to have happened in organizations in the 1980s and 1990s, is very wearing and creates cynicism amongst those it affects. There is a need to recognize that continuity, as well as change, has merits, as was noted in Chapter 1. On the other hand, it is obviously undesirable to wait until it is too late, and change is imposed by people or circumstances. Some sort of cost-benefit analysis, even in the light of various unknowns, needs to be done here.
- Can the change being envisaged be achieved? If there are serious problems, is there a better way?
- What needs to be changed and what not? It is quite easy to aim for more change than is really necessary.
- What are the potential outcomes? This may well involve scenario planning.
- Finally, what is the optimum achievable outcome? Identifying this is by no means easy, and indeed requires a vision of the future, an attribute of most successful leaders, but not something that everyone possesses.

Reflecting on the last point above, the role of leadership is a key one in change. Leadership is needed at all stages of change, and the type of leadership may be different at different stages, but it is arguably most needed when initiating and planning change. Without a vision of the future, it will be very difficult to communicate with and enthuse others about the need for change.

STAGES OF CHANGE

When a change is taking place, at any of the three levels described above, it needs to go through three critical stages if it is to have a chance of success. These stages, also identified by Kurt Lewin (1951), are:

- Unfreezing
- Changing
- Refreezing

Unfreezing

'Unfreezing' relates to the need to change existing attitudes towards working practices and processes before the change can begin to take place – it is the stage of preparing the ground. This is when communication about any proposed change is vital if people are to understand and support it. This may mean holding open meetings at which plans for change can be discussed by everyone concerned, or creating a newsletter to inform people, particularly those who may be involved and interested but who cannot attend meetings. It may mean holding one-to-one talks with key people and arranging for more widespread communication and reassurance on a cascade basis. If the change is going to involve people acquiring new skills, arrangements for training should fall into this stage as well. It is also a time when plans may need to be modified in the light of consultation with other people.

Changing

This is the implementation stage, and its success will depend on the thoroughness of your planning and preparation. In a survey of ninety-three private sector organizations where decisions, often about change, were implemented, the following conclusions were drawn:

- that the implementation stage took much longer than people expected and that time scales were often unrealistic;
- that, in many cases, major problems occurred at the stage of implementation which had not been identified at the planning stage;
- that where task forces, committees, project teams etc. were involved, co-ordination was not effective;
- that dealing with crises and problems which arose at this stage detracted from the implementation itself;
- that the skills and abilities of employees were often overestimated;
- that not enough training and instruction were provided;
- that factors outside the organization's control, such as legal, governmental or economic changes, had an adverse effect on implementation.

Although these findings suggest that careful planning can be, and often is, overturned by unforeseen events during the second stage of change, it is usually the rigidity of plans which tends to be self destructive in this way. If the situation changes, then so must the plan. There is a need for maximum flexibility in the planning and implementation of change, and change teams need to set aside time for regular reviews of progress; if this is not going according to plan, it may be necessary to change the original plans and schedules rather than try to conform to them.

Refreezing

The final stage of change is that of consolidation. Even when a change appears to have been planned and implemented successfully, problems can occur. For example, new equipment may have been effectively introduced and its operators trained in its use. Those responsible for the change, however, could pat themselves on the back too soon. Operators can too easily revert to old working practices despite the new technology unless there is ongoing monitoring once the change is in place. Not until it has become incorporated into the working culture can the change be said to have been 'refrozen'.

Refreezing, therefore, involves continuous evaluation of the success of the implementation stage. Problems or dissatisfaction may occur after implementation and these need to be identified and dealt with promptly to prevent further disruption.

RESPONSES TO CHANGE

The extent to which individuals are likely to be resistant, indifferent or supportive towards change depends on the degree to which they perceive the change will affect them personally and their way of working. People will feel threatened by change if they think it is going to affect their pay, their status, their place of work, their chances of advancement or any other aspect of their job which is important to them. They may also be resistant to change because they have suffered a surfeit of changes at work; there comes a point when people seek some kind of stability, rationally or not, in an environment of constant change.

People almost naturally appear to resist change. It seems to be part of human nature to create norms with which people feel comfortable and, if these norms are threatened, resistance occurs. Often people feel genuinely apprehensive when they hear things are likely to change, and this apprehension increases if they lack information about what is going to happen.

Kotter and Schlesinger (1979) identified the main reasons why people resisted change as:

- Parochial self-interest.
- Misunderstanding.
- Different assessments of the situation.
- Low tolerance for change.

Parochial self-interest

Subconsciously, most people put their own welfare before that of the organization. If they perceive a change as being in the organization's interests but either not in, or, worse, actively against their own interests, they will resist it. If the change, for example, is perceived to be going to result in lower pay, loss of autonomy, power, or identity, or indeed loss of any other factor of value to the individual, he or she is likely to oppose it. In addition, since most change is intended to increase efficiency, it may well be seen as requiring more work for the staff involved. This opposition, if shared with others, may result in the growth of pressure groups to prevent the change from taking place.

Misunderstanding

If communication about a proposed change has not been adequate, people are likely to misunderstand its implications for them and their jobs. If there is a lack of trust between those responsible, or held responsible, for the change and those who are going to be affected by it, misunderstanding is linked to mistrust. Rumour and conjecture are likely to result, often leading to increased resistance. This situation is likely where there are uncertainties about the proposals, or people do not have sufficient warning about what is being suggested.

Different assessments of the situation

Enthusiasts for change often assume that everyone shares their vision of its benefits. In fact, this is rarely true since individuals have different aspirations, values and expectations. Shared assessment of the benefits of change will only result if everyone is in possession of the same amount of relevant information about it. Even then, individuals may not share the same values. If the change is going to result in increased pay for everyone, for example, only those who value pay highly are likely to see this as a benefit; others may perceive disadvantages in loss of free time or reduced overtime which accompany the increase in pay. The danger in making these kinds of generalized assumptions is that there is likely to be open disagreement with the plans for change.

Low tolerance of change

If people have strong needs for security and stability, they are likely to resist change through apprehension that it will threaten these cornerstones of their existence. They may fear that they will find it difficult to learn new skills or work practices or that they may lose the companionship of their work colleagues through relocation or reallocation of work. They will oppose the idea of change, either openly or by making excuses for why they do not support it. Reassurance and support are essential for people with these apprehensions.

Investigate

> Think about a change at work in which you have been involved. Did you or your colleagues experience any resistance to change? Was this resistance caused by any of the reasons above?

Coping with reactions to change

Kotter and Schlesinger (1979) identified a number of ways by which resistance to change might be reduced, noting the advantages and disadvantages of each.

Education and communication

Educating people about the change beforehand and ensuring that ideas about change are fully communicated to everyone who is likely to be affected by it will help people to understand why the change is necessary. It is particularly effective when resistance is based on inadequate or inaccurate information and when those who are responsible for initiating the change need the support of those who oppose it. However, any adequate programme of education and communication is costly in terms of time and effort and relies on a relationship of trust between those driving and those restraining the change.

Participation and involvement

Top-down imposition of change is often unsuccessful because those designing the change have failed to take into account the knowledge and expertise of the people at whom the change is aimed. Where information from others is necessary, they need to be invited to participate in planning the change. Otherwise, they can create considerable resistance at the stage of implementation.

In general, participation and involvement of everyone who will be affected by the change leads to commitment and support for its implementation. It can, however, be an enormously time-consuming process and needs careful management. If the change needs to occur in a very short space of time, it may take too long to involve other people.

Facilitation and support

When fear and apprehension of change are the main reasons for resistance, managers need to be supportive to the problems of adjustment their staff are experiencing. They might spend time reassuring people about their apprehensions and explaining the need for change. They could also provide additional support in the form of training. All this takes time and commitment from the manager as well as patience, since fears of change may be deeply rooted and difficult to remove.

Negotiation and agreement

In some cases, opposition to change can be so powerful that incentives need to be offered if the change is to go ahead. These may take the form of individual incentives, such as promotion or a generous early retirement package, or it might involve negotiating with the union so that employees receive higher pay or other appropriate rewards in return for a change in working hours. Such negotiating tactics can prove to be expensive for the organization and a manager who resorts too easily to negotiation may be seen as a target for blackmail by other resistant groups.

Manipulation and co-option

Where, for example, an individual has considerable influence over others and, thus, power to increase resistance, managers may resort to 'co-opting' that person on to their side. This is often done by giving the person some attractive role in the design and implementation of the change so that he or she is publicly seen to be supporting it. Because it is a devious way of reducing resistance, it is also often unsuccessful and can lead to greater opposition.

Explicit and implicit coercion

As with the last method, this too is not to be recommended except as a last resort. It can involve forcing people to accept a change, riding roughshod over opposition, usually because the reasons for the change are overwhelmingly stronger than any resistance to it and, no matter what tactics are employed, the change is going to be unpopular. It requires considerable personal authority and power on the part of the person who is implementing the change as well as the ability to cope with prolonged dissatisfaction during the third stage of change.

Investigate

In the last change in which you were involved, which of the above strategies was used to achieve the change? Why was this particular strategy adopted?

With any change you are involved in planning and implementing, you can expect there to be a certain amount of resistance. The secret lies in identifying why and where this is most likely to occur and adopting a strategy in advance to cope with it. The strategy is likely to be influenced by the circumstances: the degree of resistance, the power of the initiator, and the time-scale available. At one end of the spectrum a more directive approach is likely to work where there is a clear view of what is to be done, little involvement with people, and resistance can be brushed aside; at the other end a more consultative and slower approach is indicated where there is a good deal of involvement of other people, and where there is a less definitive commitment to a particular outcome.

CHANGE AGENTS

When massive change at the organizational level needs to be undertaken, it is often necessary to bring in a 'change agent'. Organizations prefer stability and, like individuals, resist change because of the upheaval it will cause. Senior management within the organization are not usually the most adept at planning radical change since they themselves have a stake in preserving the status quo. The change agent, on the other hand, may be an independent consultant or may be recruited as a full-time member of the organization's staff.

The change agent brings a fresh and generally unbiased approach to designing a programme of change. He or she works with members of the organization at all levels, identifying the problems and helping them to generate solutions. Often, the change agent will take responsibility for implementing the solutions, particularly if they are likely to be unpopular with large sections of staff.

> David Kitchen, Personnel Director of the private health care company BUPA, describes himself as a 'change agent'. He was recruited when BUPA had just recorded a significant loss in its medical insurance division and he was given the task of replacing half the company's board and making thousands of staff redundant at a time when both the public and private health care sectors were experiencing massive changes.

A final issue in change that is all too often forgotten is evaluation of how well the change works. It is difficult because new factors start interposing themselves in the situation and interfere with any attempt to measure the outcomes of the change itself. Nevertheless, it is important to try, because there are almost certainly important lessons that can be learned and applied to the next attempt to pursue change. If evaluation is going to be successful, it is important that a process for carrying it out is built into the original plans.

Summary

Change is part of working life and every manager is likely to be involved in planning, managing or implementing change as part of his or her job. It can be seen as a threat to the status quo or as an opportunity to learn new skills and improve working practices. Pressures to change can come from outside the organization and can include social, technological, political, economic, environmental and market-related factors. They can also originate from within the organization, either from senior management who recognize the need for change or from the employees themselves.

Pressures for change can be described as the forces that drive the need for change. There are also, nearly always, opposing or restraining forces which may include financial and other resource constraints, people's reactions to proposed changes and legal or other restrictions. If these restraining forces are as strong as those driving the change, equilibrium results. In order to change the state of equilibrium, either the driving forces need to be increased or the strength of the restraining forces must be reduced.

Changes can also take place at different levels – individual, group or organizational. The level at which the change occurs will be directly related to the expected degree of difficulty you are likely to encounter in implementing it, and the length of time it will take to put it into place.

Planning and implementing change usually requires a three-stage approach consisting of unfreezing existing work practices and attitudes, changing to new practices and refreezing these as part of organizational, group and individual working culture.

There is a tendency for people to resist change owing to their own perceptions that change is likely to affect them adversely. Often, they are not fully aware of why the change is necessary and this is usually the result of poor communication between managers and their staff. A number of ways to reduce resistance to change have been suggested, including better education of, and communication with, everyone affected by it, increasing participation and involvement, providing support for natural apprehension about change and the offering of incentives. Finally, there may be a role for the 'change agent', who may be brought into an organization to effect radical change.

Activities

This may involve consolidating some of the answers to investigations as you went through the chapter. Think of a change at work in which you were personally involved.

1   Identify:
    (a) any external pressures for change;
    (b) any internal pressures for change.
2   At which level(s) did the change take place:
    (a) individual;
    (b) group;
    (c) organizational?
3   Draw a forcefield analysis of the change, identifying the driving and restraining forces and indicating their relative strengths.
4   What amount of preparatory analysis was carried out?
5   What efforts were made to:
    (a) unfreeze the change;
    (b) effect the change;
    (c) refreeze or consolidate the change?
6   Was there any resistance to the idea of change or to the change itself? What were the underlying causes of this resistance?
7   What methods were used to reduce or overcome any resistance to change?
8   Was there any evaluation of the change after the event?

REFERENCES

Advisory, Conciliation and Arbitration Service (ACAS), *Annual Reports*, London

Advisory, Conciliation and Arbitration Service (ACAS) (2001) *Advisory Handbook* 'Discipline and Grievances at Work', London

Adair, J. (1983) *Effective Leadership*, Pan Books, London

Adair, J. (1987) *How to Manage your Time*, Talbot-Adair/McGraw-Hill

Baddeley, S. and James, K. (1987) 'Owl, Fox, Donkey, Sheep: Political Skills for Managers', *Management Education and Development*, **18**, 3–9

Bedell, G. (1992) 'You're fired!' *The Independent on Sunday*, 31 May, p. 18

Belbin, R. M. (1981, latest edition 1991) *Management Teams: Why They Succeed or Fail*, Butterworth-Heinemann, Oxford

Belbin, R. M. (1993) *The Management of Team Roles*, Butterworth-Heinemann, Oxford

Bevan, S. and Thompson, M. (1992) 'An Overview of Policy and Practice' in *Performance Management in the UK*, Institute of Personnel and Development, London

Bouwen, R. and Salipante, P. F. (1990) Behavioural analysis of grievances: episodes, actions and outcomes. *Employee Relations (UK)*, **12**(4), 27–32

Boyatzis, R. (1982) *The Competent Manager*, John Wiley and Sons, New York

Dawson, S. (1992) *Analysing Organizations*, 2nd edn, Macmillan, London

Drucker, P. (1954) *The Practice of Management*, Harper and Row, New York

Fayol, H. (1949 [1916]) *General and Industrial Management* (trans. Storrs), Pitman, London

Fletcher, C. and Williams, R. (1992) 'Organizational Experiences' in *Performance Management in the UK*, Institute of Personnel and Development, London

Fox, S. and McLeay, S. (1991) An Approach to Researching Managerial Labour Markets: HRM, Corporate Strategy and Financial Performance in UK Manufacturing, *British Academy of Management Annual Conference*, Bath University

Fraser, M. (1978) *Employment Interviewing*, MacDonald and Evans, London

Gospel, H. (1992) 'Management Structure and Strategies: An Introduction' in Gospel, H. and Littler, C. (eds) *Management Strategies and Industrial Relations*, Heinemann, London

Guest, D., Michie, J., Sheehan, M. and Conway, N. (2000) *Employment Relations, HRM and Business Performance*, Chartered Institute of Personnel and Development, London

Hackman, J. R. and Oldham, G. R. (1976) Motivation through the design of work: test of a theory. *Organizational Behaviour and Human Performance*, **16**, 250–79

Handy, C. (1993) *Understanding Organizations*, Penguin, Harmondsworth

Herriot, P. and Pemberton, C. (1995) *Competitive Advantage Through Diversity*, Sage, London

Herzberg, F. (1968) One more time: how do you motivate employees? *Harvard Business Review*, **46**, 53–62

Herzberg, F., Mausner, B. and Snyderman, B. B. (1959) *The Motivation to Work*, John Wiley, New York

Hofstede, G. (1980) *Culture's Consequences: International Differences in Work Related Values*, Sage, London

Hunt, J. W. (1979) *Managing People at Work*, McGraw-Hill, Maidenhead

Huselid, M (1995) The Impact of Human Resource Management Practices on Turnover, Productivity and Corporate Financial Performance. *Academy of Management Journal*, **40**, 171–88

Iles, P. (2001) 'Resourcing', in Storey, J. (ed.) [in] Human Resource Management: A Critical Text (Second Edition), Thomson Learning, London

Institute of Personnel and Development, Continuous Development: People and Work (regularly published), *Institute of Personnel Management Code of Practice*, IPD, London

International Labour Organization (1965) *International Labour Conference Report*, **7**(1): Examination of Grievances and Communications within the Undertaking, ILO, Geneva, pp. 7–9

James, K. and Burgoyne, J. (2001) *Leadership Development: Best Practice Guide for Organizations*, Council for Excellence in Management and Leadership, London

Janis, I. L. (1982) *Groupthink*, Houghton-Mifflin, Boston, Mass.

Kandola, R. and Fullerton, J. (1994) Diversity: more than just an empty slogan, *Personnel Management*, Nov., pp. 46–50

Kennedy, P. (1993) *Preparing for the Twenty-first Century*, HarperCollins, London

Koontz, H. (1962) Making Sense of Management Theory, *Harvard Business Review*, **40**(4)

Kotter, J. P. and Schlesinger, L. A. (1979) Choosing strategies for change, *Harvard Business Review*, March/April

Kotter, J. (1995) *The New Rules: How to Succeed in Today's Post-Corporate World*, Free Press, New York

Lewin, K. (1951) *Field Theory in Social Science*, Harper, London

McGregor, D. (1960) *The Human Side of Enterprise*, McGraw-Hill, London

McKevitt, D. and Lawton, A. (1996) The Manager, the Citizen, the Politician and Performance Measures. *Public Money and Management*, July–September, 49–54

Mabey, C. and Thomson, A. (2000) *Achieving Management Excellence: A Survey of UK Management Development at the Millennium*, Institute of Management, London

Maslow, A. H. (1943) A theory of human motivation. *Psychological Review*, 50

Merrick, N. (1995) The Mobil way to achieve mobility, *People Management*, Nov., pp. 37–8

Moss Kanter, R. (1992) *The Change Masters*, Routledge, London

Mumford, A. (1997) *Management Development* (Third Edition), Institute of Personnel and Development, London

O'Neill, B. (2000) *Test Your Leadership Skills*, Institute of Management, London

Parkinson, C. N. (1986) *Parkinson's Law*, Harmondsworth, Penguin

Patterson, M. *et al.* (1997) *Impact of People Management Practices on Business Performance*, Institute of Personnel and Development, London

Pearson, R. (1991) *The Human Resource: Managing People and Work in the 1990s*, McGraw-Hill, Maidenhead

Pinder, T. H. (1980) Effective speaking. *Occupational Therapy*, May

Pugh, D. S. and Hickson, D. J. (1996) *Writers on Organizations*, Penguin Business Books, Harmondsworth

Randell, G. (1984) *Staff Appraisal*, Institute of Personnel and Development

Reddy, M. (1987) *The Manager's Guide to Counselling*, British Psychological Society/Methuen, London

Rodger, A. (1952) *The Seven Point Plan*, National Institute of Industrial Psychology, Paper No. 1

Rowntree, D. (1988) *The Manager's Book of Checklists*, Corgi Books

Schein, E. (1978) *Career Dynamics: Matching Individual and Organizational Needs*, Addison-Wesley, Reading, Mass.

Schuler, R. (2001) 'International Human Resource Management' in Storey, J. (ed.) *Human Resource Management: A Critical View* (Second Edition) Thomson Learning, London

Simon, H. A. (1960) *The New Science of Management Decision*, Harper and Row

Stewart, R. (1982) *Choices for the Manager*, McGraw-Hill

Storey, J (2001) 'Human Resource Management Today: An Assessment', in Storey, J. (ed.) *Human Resource Management: A Critical Text* (Second Edition) Thomson Learning, London

Taylor, F. W. (1947) *Scientific Management*, Harper and Row, New York

Theaker, M. (1995) *Entering the era of electronic CVs, People Management*, August, pp. 34–7

Thomson, A. W. J. and Murray, V. V. (1976) *Grievance Procedures*, Saxon House/Lexington Books, Farnborough (UK)/Lexington, Mass., pp. 17–18

Tuckman, B. W. (1965) Development sequences in small groups. *Psychological Bulletin*, 63

Warr, P. B. (1987) *Work, Unemployment and Mental Health*, Oxford University Press

Wellins, R. S. (1992) 'Building a self-directed work team', *Training and Development*, December, pp. 24–8.

Woodcock, M. (1989) *Team Development Manual*, Gower, London

Woodcock, M. and Francis, D. (1990) *Organization Development through Teambuilding*, Gower, London

Wrightsman, L. S. (1974) *Assumptions about Human Nature*, Brooks/Cole, Monterey, Ca.

FURTHER READING

There is of course an immense literature in this area, but the following are valuable sources of reference:

Advisory, Conciliation, and Arbitration Service (ACAS) publications, notably:

> Job evaluation: an introduction
> Pay systems
> Recruitment and induction
> Employee communications and consultation
> Employee appraisal
> Effective organizations: the people factor
> Teamwork: success through people
> Discipline and grievances at work

Armstrong, M. (2001) *A Handbook of Human Resource Management Practice* (Eighth Edition), Kogan Page, London

Lewis, D. and Sargeant, M. (2000) *Essentials of Employment Law*, Chartered Institute of Personnel and Development, London.

Index